# Reading 3
## without answers

## Liz Driscoll

CAMBRIDGE
UNIVERSITY PRESS

CAMBRIDGE UNIVERSITY PRESS
Cambridge, New York, Melbourne, Madrid, Cape Town, Singapore, São Paulo, Delhi

Cambridge University Press
The Edinburgh Building, Cambridge CB2 8RU, UK

www.cambridge.org
Information on this title: www.cambridge.org/9780521705745

First published 2008

Printed in the United Kingdom at the University Press, Cambridge

A catalogue record for this publication is available from the British Library

ISBN-13  978-0-521-70574-5

# Contents

# Map of the book

| Unit number | Title | Topic | How to ... |
|---|---|---|---|
| 9 | **Safety at work** | Fire regulations | <ul><li>work out the meaning of unknown words from the context</li><li>understand a leaflet about preventing a fire</li><li>follow instructions for a fire drill</li></ul> |
| 10 | **Lines of communication** | Emails and notices at work | <ul><li>work out who an email is from and who it is to</li><li>work out the main purpose of an email</li><li>understand resignation and appointment notices</li></ul> |
| 11 | **Any comments?** | Questionnaires and feedback | <ul><li>interpret a completed questionnaire</li><li>distinguish between comments and suggested action</li><li>understand how writers link facts and ideas</li></ul> |
| 12 | **I'm going to apply** | Job applications | <ul><li>understand a job advertisement</li><li>distinguish between formal and informal language</li><li>understand an offer of employment and confirm acceptance</li></ul> |
| 13 | **I'm off on a trip** | Business travel research | <ul><li>interpret statistics</li><li>interpret charts and graphs</li><li>find out about business etiquette in another country</li></ul> |
| 14 | **Look it up!** | Using reference materials | <ul><li>find information in a reference book</li><li>use reference books to complete a crossword</li><li>find answers to questions in a reference book</li></ul> |
| 15 | **It's on the shelf** | Using a library database | <ul><li>understand instructions in a library catalogue</li><li>understand what a novel is about from the blurb</li><li>read fiction without worrying about difficult language</li></ul> |
| 16 | **Read about reading** | The process of reading | <ul><li>skim a text and identify the main points</li><li>identify the topic of each paragraph within a text</li><li>relate what you have read to your own experiences</li></ul> |

**Work and Study**

# Acknowledgements

I would particularly like to thank Ros Henderson, of Cambridge University Press, for her support and guidance in the writing of this book, as well as for her superb editing. I am also very grateful to Brigit Viney for her wonderful comments and suggestions, to Nóirín Burke, who commissioned the project, and to Linda Matthews for overseeing its production.

My thanks go to Stephanie White and Paul Fellows at Kamae Design for their creative design work.

I am also grateful to Bill Henman, Ian Lees, Marcos Martos Higueras, Jane Read, Marina Rose, Richard Walker and Mary Yoe for their help in finding the texts.

The author and publishers are grateful to the following reviewers for their valuable insights and suggestions:

Steve Banfield, United Arab Emirates; Ildiko Berke, Hungary; Ian Chisholm, UK; Alper Darici, Turkey; Helen Dixon, UK; Rosie Ganne, UK; Jean Greenwood, UK; Elif Isler, Turkey; Kathy Kolarik, Australia; L. Krishnaveni, Malaysia; Beatriz Martín, Spain; Steve Miller, UK; Ersoy Osman, UK

The authors and publishers acknowledge the following sources of copyright material and are grateful for the permissions granted. While every effort has been made, it has not always been possible to identify the sources of all the material used, or to trace all copyright holders. If any omissions are brought to our notice, we will be happy to include the appropriate acknowledgements on reprinting.

pp. 10–11: National Magazine Company for recipe 'Pasta with aubergine and mozzarella sauce' from *Good Housekeeping Complete Book of Pasta;* pp. 14–16: Avis for the car rental voucher and material from their website, © 2000–2007 AVIS Rent A Car; pp. 22–23: Air Canada for webpages, checked baggage allowance and excess baggage fees, www.aircanada.com; pp. 26–27: Royal Mail 'Sorry, you were out' card and 'Making Redelivery easy' text from www.royalmail.com Reproduced by kind permission of Royal Mail Group Ltd. All Rights Reserved.; p. 28: Thames Water for 'Interruptions to your water supply' card, © 2007 Thames Water Utilities; pp. 31–33: Ceri and Elaine Morgan for Ramsey House letter and website material from www.stayinwales.co.uk; p. 35: article 'Call of the Wild' from *Horizons* The Magazine of Explore!, June 2006, by permission of Sandy Beatty of Explore! (www.explore.co.uk); pp. 36–37: *Getaway* magazine for the article 'A walk in the park', August 2004; p. 39: *The Times* for article by Jeremy Whittle, 'Cooke shows ingredients for big prize', 20 September 2006, © N I Syndication; p. 39: article 'Cyclists facing £2,500 bell fines' by Tim Shipman, *Daily Mail*, 11 September 2006 and p. 40: 'Cyclists with helmets "more like to be hit"' by Ray Massey, *Daily Mail*, 12 September 2006, © Associated Newspapers Ltd; p. 39: article 'The bicycle that turned into folding money' by Ben Laurance, *Observer*, 7 August 2005; p. 43: text from Excess Baggage brochure, Excess Baggage Group Ltd; p. 43: Southern Electric 'call- back' card, © Scottish and Southern Energy Group; p. 44: Merricks Media Ltd for text 'New beginning' by Amanda Hemmings, *Australia and New Zealand*, August and September 2006; p. 47: The Midcounties Co-operative for text 'Help prevent fire' and p. 81: 'Slips, trips and falls are a danger to you and your customers', Scriptographic Publications Ltd; p. 48: Cambridge University Press for fire drill procedure; pp. 66–67: for entries for 'brass', 'lycra', 'metal' from *Cambridge Advanced Learner's Dictionary, 2nd Edition*, 2005; pp. 66–67: entries for 'ground' and 'mental' from *Cambridge Idioms Dictionary, 2nd Edition*, 2006; p. 70: entry for 'fiction' and pp. 92–95: all entries from *Cambridge Learner's Dictionary, 3rd Edition*, 2004, © Cambridge University Press, reproduced with permission; pp. 66–67: entries for 'follower' and 'stare' from *Penguin Reference Pocket Thesaurus*, edited by Rosalind Fergusson, Martin Manser and David Pickering, Penguin Books, 2004, © Penguin Group UK; pp. 66–67: definitions 'Laurel and Hardy', 'Channel Islands' and 'insect' from *Hutchinson Encyclopedia*, 2001, Helicon, RM Education plc; pp. 68–69: extracts from the *Chambers Book of Facts*, © Chambers 2005. Reproduced by permission of Chambers Harrap Publishers Ltd; pp. 70–71: Oxfordshire County Council for adapted text 'Library Catalogue Help', www.libcat.oxfordshire.gov.uk; p. 73: text from *4.50 from Paddington* by Agatha Christie, and p. 79: extract from *Death on the Nile* by Agatha Christie, published by HarperCollins, © Agatha Christie Ltd; pp. 74–76: text 'Reading' excerpted from *The World Book Encyclopedia*, © 2007. By permission of the publisher: www.worldbookonline.com; p. 79: extract 'Wanted: a computer, female aged 18–25' from *Much Ado About English: Up and Down the Bizarre Byways of a Fascinating Language* by Richard Watson Todd, Nicholas Brealey Publishing; p. 79: tables 'Watches and clocks: exports 2002– 2005' and 'Watches and clocks: imports 2002–2005', © International Trade Centre, 2007; p. 81: Usdaw for texts 'Should first aid be provided in my workplace?' and 'Can my employer stop me putting entries into the accident book?' from www.usdaw.org.uk

The publishers are grateful to the following for permission to reproduce copyright photographs and material:

Key: l = left, c = centre, r = right, t = top, b = bottom

Alamy/©Andrew Butterton for p. 26 /©Afripics.com for p. 36 /©Louise Murray for p. 37 /©Photofusion Picture Library for p. 40 /©A M Corporation for p. 54 /©Asia Images Group for p. 64 /©Ian Shaw for p. 74 (t) /©Kitt Cooper-Smith for p. 77; Britain on View for p. 30; Corbis Images/©Jon Hicks for p. 14; News International Syndication for p. 39 (l); Photolibrary/©PhotoDisc for p. 35; Punchstock/©Image Source for p. 33 /©Bananastock for p. 50 /©Digital Vision for p. 58 /©Comstock for p. 71 /©Image Source for p. 74 (b); Shutterstock/©TT Photo for p. 39 (r); Tourism Australia /©Nino Ellison for p. 44.

Front cover of *The Penguin Reference Pocket Thesaurus* edited by Rosalind Fergusson, Martin Manser and David Pickering (Penguin Books, 2004) on p. 66 (3) copyright ©Penguin Books Ltd, 2004.

Front cover of *The Hutchinson Concise Encyclopaedia* on p. 66 (2) Copyright © RM Education plc.

Cover of *4.50 From Paddington* on p. 72 ©1957 Agatha Christie Limited, a Chorion company, all rights reserved.

Illustrations:

Kathy Baxendale pp. 29, 30, 40, 62, 63; Mark Duffin pp. 11, 12, 23, 24, 25, 43, 46, 52, 65; Laura Martinez p. 19; Rory Walker p. 22.

**Text design and page make-up:** Kamae Design, Oxford
**Cover design:** Kamae Design, Oxford
**Cover photo:** © Getty Images
**Picture research:** Hilary Luckcock

# Introduction
## To the student

### Who is *Real Reading 3* for?

You can use this book if you are a student at intermediate or upper-intermediate level and you want to improve your English reading. You can use the book alone without a teacher or you can use it in a classroom with a teacher.

### How will *Real Reading 3* help me with my reading?

*Real Reading 3* contains texts for everyday reading practice, for example leaflets, notices, websites, newspapers, etc. It is designed to help you with reading you will need to do in English at home or when visiting another country.

The exercises in each unit help you develop useful skills such as working out the meaning of unknown words from context and ignoring parts of the text which are not useful to you. *Real Reading 3* discourages you from using a dictionary to find out the meaning of every word you do not know.

### How is *Real Reading 3* organized?

The book has 16 units and is divided into two sections:
- Units 1–8 – social and travel situations
- Units 9–16 – work and study situations

Every unit is divided into Reading A and Reading B and has:
- *Get ready to read*: to introduce you to the topic of the unit
- *Learning tip*: to help you improve your learning
- *Class bonus*: an exercise you can do with other students or friends
- *Focus on*: to help you study useful grammar or vocabulary
- *Did you know?*: extra information about vocabulary, different cultures or the topic of the unit
- *Extra practice*: an extra exercise for more practice
- *Can-do checklist*: to help you think about what you learnt in the unit.

After each section there is a review unit. The reviews help you practise the skills you learn in each section.

At the back of the book you can find:
- *Appendices*: contain lists of *Useful language*, *Learning tips* for every unit and information about *Using a dictionary*.

### How can I use *Real Reading 3*?

The units at the end of the book are more difficult than the units at the beginning of the book. However, you do not need to do the units in order. It is better to choose the units that are most interesting for you and to do them in the order you prefer.

There are many different ways you can use this book. We suggest you work in this way:
- Look in the *Contents* list and find a unit that interests you.
- Prepare yourself for reading by working through the *Get ready to read* exercises.
- Look at *Appendix 1: Useful language* for the unit.
- Do the exercises in Reading A. Use the example answers to guide you. Put the *Learning tip* into practice (either in Reading A or Reading B).
- Do the exercises in Reading B.
- Check your answers with your teacher.
- If you want to do more work, do the *Extra practice* activity.
- At the end of the unit, think about what you have learnt and complete the *Can-do checklist*.
- Look at the list of *Learning tips* in *Appendix 2* and decide which other tips you have used in the unit.

# Introduction
## To the teacher

### What is *Cambridge English Skills*?

*Real Reading 3* is one of 12 books in the *Cambridge English Skills* series. The series also contains *Real Writing* and *Real Listening & Speaking* books and offers skills training to students from elementary to advanced level. All the books are available in with-answers and without-answers editions.

| Level | Book | Author |
|---|---|---|
| Elementary<br>CEF: A2<br>Cambridge ESOL: KET<br>NQF Skills for life: Entry 2 | Real Reading 1 with answers | Liz Driscoll |
| | Real Reading 1 without answers | Liz Driscoll |
| | Real Writing 1 with answers and audio CD | Graham Palmer |
| | Real Writing 1 without answers | Graham Palmer |
| | Real Listening & Speaking 1 with answers and audio CDs (2) | Miles Craven |
| | Real Listening & Speaking 1 without answers | Miles Craven |
| Pre-intermediate<br>CEF: B1<br>Cambridge ESOL: PET<br>NQF Skills for life: Entry 3 | Real Reading 2 with answers | Liz Driscoll |
| | Real Reading 2 without answers | Liz Driscoll |
| | Real Writing 2 with answers and audio CD | Graham Palmer |
| | Real Writing 2 without answers | Graham Palmer |
| | Real Listening & Speaking 2 with answers and audio CDs (2) | Sally Logan & Craig Thaine |
| | Real Listening & Speaking 2 without answers | Sally Logan & Craig Thaine |
| Intermediate to upper-intermediate<br>CEF: B2<br>Cambridge ESOL: FCE<br>NQF Skills for life: Level 1 | Real Reading 3 with answers | Liz Driscoll |
| | Real Reading 3 without answers | Liz Driscoll |
| | Real Writing 3 with answers and audio CD | Roger Gower |
| | Real Writing 3 without answers | Roger Gower |
| | Real Listening & Speaking 3 with answers and audio CDs (2) | Miles Craven |
| | Real Listening & Speaking 3 without answers | Miles Craven |
| Advanced<br>CEF: C1<br>Cambridge ESOL: CAE<br>NQF Skills for life: Level 2 | Real Reading 4 with answers | Liz Driscoll |
| | Real Reading 4 without answers | Liz Driscoll |
| | Real Writing 4 with answers and audio CD | Simon Haines |
| | Real Writing 4 without answers | Simon Haines |
| | Real Listening & Speaking 4 with answers and audio CDs (2) | Miles Craven |
| | Real Listening & Speaking 4 without answers | Miles Craven |

## Where are the teacher's notes?

The series is accompanied by a dedicated website containing detailed teaching notes and extension ideas for every unit of every book. Please visit www.cambridge.org/englishskills to access the *Cambridge English Skills* teacher's notes.

## What are the main aims of *Real Reading 3*?

- To help students develop reading skills in accordance with the ALTE (Association of Language Testers in Europe) Can-do statements. These statements describe what language users can typically do at different levels and in different contexts. Visit www.alte.org for further information.
- To encourage autonomous learning by focusing on learner training.

## What are the key features of *Real Reading 3*?

- It is aimed at intermediate and upper-intermediate learners of English at levels B1–B2 of the Council of Europe's CEFR (Common European Framework of Reference for Languages).
- It contains 16 four-page units, divided into two sections: Social and Travel, and Work and Study.
- *Real Reading 3* units are divided into Reading A and Reading B and contain:
  - *Get ready to read* warm-up exercises to get students thinking about the topic
  - *Learning tips* which give students advice on how to improve their reading and their learning
  - *Class bonus* communication activities for pairwork and group work so that you can adapt the material to suit your class
  - *Focus on* exercises which provide contextualized practice in particular language or vocabulary areas
  - *Did you know?* boxes which provide notes on cultural or linguistic differences between English-speaking countries, or factual information on the topic of the unit
  - *Extra practice* extension tasks which provide more real world reading practice
  - *Can-do checklists* at the end of every unit to encourage students to think about what they have learnt.
- There are two review units to practise skills that have been introduced in the units.
- It has an international feel and contains a range of texts from English-speaking countries.
- It can be used as self-study material, in class, or as supplementary homework material.

## What is the best way to use *Real Reading 3* in the classroom?

The book is designed so that the units may be used in any order, although the more difficult units naturally appear near the end of the book, in the *Work and Study* section.

You can consult the unit-by-unit teacher's notes at www.cambridge.org/englishskills for detailed teaching ideas. However, broadly speaking, different parts of the book can be approached in the following ways:

- *Useful language*: You can use the *Useful language* lists in *Appendix 1* to preteach or revise the vocabulary from the unit you are working on.
- *Get ready to read*: It is a good idea to use this section as an introduction to the topic. Students can work on the exercises in pairs or groups. Many of these require students to answer questions about their personal experience. These questions can be used as prompts for discussion. Some exercises contain a problem-solving element that students can work on together. Other exercises aim to clarify key vocabulary in the unit. You can present these vocabulary items directly to students.
- *Learning tips*: You can ask students to read and discuss these in an open-class situation. An alternative approach is for you to create a series of discussion questions associated with the *Learning tip*. Students can discuss their ideas in pairs or small groups followed by open-class feedback. The *Learning tip* acts as a reflective learning tool to help promote learner autonomy.
- *Class bonuses*: The material in these activities aims to provide freer practice. You can set these up carefully, then take the role of observer during the activity so that students carry out the task freely. You can make yourself available to help students or analyze the language they produce during the activity.
- *Extra practice*: These activities can be set as homework or out-of-class projects for your students. Alternatively, students can do some activities in pairs during class time.
- *Can-do checklists*: Refer to these at the beginning of a lesson to explain to students what the lesson will cover, and again at the end so that students can evaluate their learning for themselves.
- *Appendices*: You may find it useful to refer your students to the *Useful language*, *Learning tips* and *Using a dictionary* sections. Students can use these as general checklists to help them with their reading.

# Unit 1
# I'll cook something

go to Useful language p. 82

○ Circle the words in these sentences so that they are true for you.
   I prefer to buy *locally produced / organic / cheap* food.
   I usually buy *fresh / ready-made / frozen* food.
   I usually do my shopping *in a supermarket / at a market / online*.
   I *never / hardly ever / often* cook for friends.
   I like trying new recipes from *my own country / my own and one or two other countries / all over the world*.

○ Match the beginnings and endings of these sentences.
   a   Bolognese sauce          is made from peanut butter, garlic, vinegar and chilli peppers.
   b   Béchamel sauce           is made from sugar, soy sauce and rice vinegar.
   c   Satay sauce              is made from minced beef, carrot and tomato puree.
   d   Sweet and sour sauce     is made from flour, butter and milk.

○ Do you know where each of the sauces above comes from?

## A   What should I make?

1   You want to cook for some friends and decide to compare some recipes. Look at these three sets of ingredients and find a pasta dish that uses tinned tomatoes, garlic and Parmesan cheese. (You like this combination of flavours.)

### Pasta with aubergine and green pepper sauce

(SERVES 4)
1 large aubergine, diced
1 onion, chopped
2 tbsp olive oil
1 garlic clove, crushed
1 green pepper, de-seeded and chopped
1 tbsp fresh basil
225 g tomatoes, skinned and chopped
salt and black pepper
400 g pasta
4 tbsp freshly grated Parmesan cheese

### Pasta with fresh tomato and olive sauce

(serves 4)

**4 large ripe tomatoes**

**125 g stoned black Greek-style olives, roughly chopped**

**2 garlic cloves, peeled and finely chopped**

**4 tbsp fresh basil, chopped**

**150 ml olive oil**

**salt and black pepper**

**400 g pasta**

### Pasta with aubergine and mozzarella sauce

90 ml olive oil
1 onion, peeled and chopped
2 garlic cloves, peeled and crushed
1 medium aubergine, about 400 g, diced
400 g can chopped tomatoes
salt and black pepper
15 g fresh basil leaves, shredded
150 g mozzarella cheese, diced
2 tbsp pine nuts
4 tbsp freshly grated Parmesan cheese
400 g pasta

(serves 4)

ml = millilitre     g = gram     tsp = teaspoon     tbsp = tablespoon

## Focus on ...
### verbs

ab c def

Look at the pictures. Circle the correct word in each pair.

Match these pictures with the verbs you did not use.

a  stone / chop
b  peel / shred

c  crush / de-seed
d  dice / grate

e  ............................
f  ............................

g  ............................
h  ............................

---

**2 You already have olive oil, garlic and pine nuts. What else do you need to make the pasta dish you chose in Exercise 1? Make a list.**

............................................................
............................................................
............................................................

**3 Read the instructions for making the dish you chose in Exercise 1. Are the statements below true (T) or false (F)?**

**1** Fry the onion, garlic and aubergine for 8–10 minutes in the olive oil.
**2** Add the tomatoes and seasoning. Bring to the boil, lower the heat and simmer for 15 minutes.
**3** Meanwhile, cook the pasta in plenty of salted water until *al dente*.
**4** Drain the pasta, and mix with the tomato and aubergine sauce. Add the basil, mozzarella and pine nuts, and mix well.
**5** Serve at once, with the Parmesan handed out separately.

a  You fry the aubergine.  _T_
b  You cook the pasta at the same time as the sauce. ......
c  You need to use the mozzarella before the tomatoes. ......
d  You add the Parmesan before serving. ......
e  You need to cook the pine nuts before you add them to the pasta. ......

**4 You want to make an Italian dessert to go with your pasta dish. A friend has given you this recipe for tiramisù. Read it and add the ingredients you need to the shopping list.**

Tiramisù
1  Cover bottom of dish with sponge fingers (about 15). Soak with strong fresh coffee.
2  Separate 3 eggs. Beat egg whites until firm.
3  Mix 250 g mascarpone into egg whites.
4  Add egg yolks and 2 tbsp sugar, and mix. Pour over sponge fingers.
5  Sieve 1 tsp cocoa powder over mixture.
6  Cover and leave in fridge overnight before serving.

DON'T FORGET TO BUY

sponge fingers (about 15)
............................................................
............................................................
............................................................
............................................................

## Did you know ...?

Tiramisù is an Italian dish and its name means 'pick me up'. The dessert could be a *pick-me-up* – something which will make you feel better. Or perhaps you will need someone to *pick you up* – lift you – after you have eaten it because it is so rich.

# B Which one should I buy?

1 You are going to make pasta with aubergine and mozzarella sauce and tiramisù for three friends. Look again at the lists of ingredients you made in Exercises 2 and 4 on page 11.

2 You are in the supermarket choosing the ingredients you need. Look quickly at the labels on these pages and decide which dish each pair of products is for.

Pasta with aubergine and mozzarella sauce  1a and 1b

.......................................................................................................

Tiramisù  .......................................................................................................

**1a**

69p

**egg penne**
delicious fresh egg pasta

Cooking time 3 MINUTES
Display until 05 JUL
Use by 07 JULY

250 g

**1b**

high in fibre

59p

**wholewheat penne**
made from 100% durum wheat

Store in a cool place.
Allow 50 - 75g of pasta per person
for a starter, 75 - 100g for a main course.
Add salt and simmer for 10 - 12 minutes.

500 g

**2a**

DISPLAY UNTIL 23 JUNE
BEST BEFORE 30 JUNE  86p

**HEDGEROW FARM**

6 large barn eggs
laid by hens in large barns

**2b**

6 eggs from hens which are free to roam outdoors and whose diet contains grains which are not genetically modified

MEDIUM

DISPLAY UNTIL 20 JUNE
BEST BEFORE 27 JUNE

89p

L

**3a**

35 g

**Black Peppercorns**
Use whole or grind in a pepper mill

£1.38

**3b**

£1.55

**Ground Black Pepper**

Ideal for savoury dishes

33 g

**4a**

£2.11

Extra mature Parmesan From Italy
**Fresh grated Parmigiano Reggiano**

Full Flavour

120 gram

**4b**

**Grated Italian**
Suitable for all pasta dishes
**Hard Cheese**

partially dried Italian hard cheese

99p  80 gram

**5a**

Keep it fresh easy reseleable pack

Colombian
**Coffee beans**

for grinding medium roasted suitable for all machines

227 gram e  £2.25

**5b**

10 cup - size

**Coffee filters**
ground coffee medium

£1.95

How to serve
Shake the filter and rest it on the cup.

Pour in freshly boiled water and leave for 3 - 4 minutes.

**6a**

58p  **Italian**
**PLUM TOMATOES**
in tasty tomato juice

400 g

**6b**

**Quality CHOPPED TOMATOES**
A new packaging
This carton is safe and light, and easy to open, pour and store

45p

390 gram

## Learning tip

We always read for a purpose. Sometimes this means that we do not need to read everything in front of us in order to find the information we are looking for. We can ignore some of the text.

**3** Look again at the product labels and think about the advantages and disadvantages of each item in each pair. Use a chart to make notes about cost, quality, preparation time and equipment needed.

| | Ingredient | Advantages | Disadvantages |
|---|---|---|---|
| 1a | egg penne | cooks in 3 minutes | expensive, packet too small for 4 people |
| 1b | wholewheat penne | healthier, cheaper, bigger packet | takes longer to cook |
| 2a | | | |
| 2b etc. | | | |

**4** Now decide which product from each pair you are going to buy. What are your reasons?

## Class bonus

Work in small groups. Discuss your choices. Have you chosen the same products?

**5** Look at the till receipt below. Did you choose the same products as this shopper?

```
QUAL CHPPD TOM                       £0.45
CASTER SUGAR                         £0.59
SPONGE FINGER                        £0.79
WHOLEWHEAT PENNE                     £0.59
MEDIUM EGGS X6                       £0.89
GRD B/PEPPR                          £1.55
COCOA                                £2.29
GRATED PARMESAN                      £2.11
ROCKET SALAD                         £1.64
DRY BLK OLIVES                       £1.05
MOZZARELLA BAG                       £1.09
AUBERGINE                            £0.99
BUNCH BASIL                          £0.75
ONIONS LOOSE 0.3 KG @ 0.73/KG        £0.22
COFFEE FILTER                        £1.95
TABLE SALT BOTTLE                    £0.30
ORGANIC BREAD                        £1.35
FRUIT JUICE 1L              2 @ £1.99
                                     £3.98

BALANCE DUE                         £22.58
CASH                                £30.00
CHANGE DUE                           £7.42
```

**6** What else did this shopper buy in order to make pasta with aubergine and mozzarella sauce and tiramisù? Circle the purchases on the till receipt.

## E X tra practice

Have a look in your kitchen cupboards at home. Have any of the packets got ingredients or instructions in English? The next time you go shopping, buy something with instructions in English. Try and follow the English instructions when you use the ingredients.

## Can-do checklist

Tick what you can do.

| | Can do | Need more practice |
|---|---|---|
| I can find information in a text without reading every word. | | |
| I can understand detailed information in a recipe. | | |
| I can choose products from their labels. | | |
| I can understand a till receipt. | | |

# Unit 2
# We've hired a car

go to Useful language p. 82

## Get ready to read

- How do people usually travel around when they visit your country on holiday?
  Tick ✓ one or more of the boxes.
  boat ☐  bus ☐  car ☐  plane ☐  train ☐

- Add *never* to these sentences where necessary to make them true for you.
  I've ..................... been abroad on holiday.
  I've ..................... flown to a holiday destination.
  I've ..................... driven a hire car on holiday.
  I've ..................... collected a hire car from the airport.

- In this unit, you are going to read about two people who are going to South Africa on holiday. Which of these cities are in South Africa? Tick ✓ one or more of the boxes.
  Abuja ☐  Cape Town ☐  Durban ☐  Johannesburg ☐  Nairobi ☐

## A Terms and conditions

1 **Claudio and Flavia Martinuzzo are going on holiday to South Africa. They have arranged car hire with Avis and have received the car rental voucher below. Look at the voucher and (circle) the cities to make a correct sentence.**

They are collecting the car from *Cape Town / Durban / Johannesburg* and they are returning it to *Cape Town / Durban / Johannesburg*.

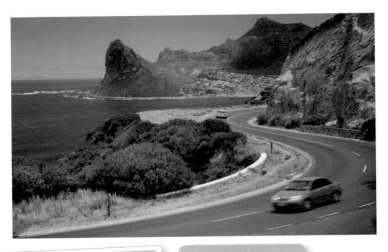

### Learning tip

We sometimes search a text for a specific piece of information – this could be the answer to a question or simply a particular word or words. This type of reading is called scanning. When we scan, we do not read every word. We look quickly to find what we are looking for. Scanning may be the first step in our reading of a text. Once we have found something we are looking for, we might go on to read the text around it.

**AVIS** CAR RENTAL VOUCHER

| | |
|---|---|
| RENTER'S NAME | ISSUED BY |
| MR C MARTINUZZO | |
| VOUCHER NUMBER 3729656-0 | DATE ISSUED 11JUL |
| RENTAL LOCATION CPT DOWNTOWN | RESERVATION NUMBER 39073636GBO |
| RENTAL DATE 30 AUG | RENTAL LENGTH 20 days | CAR GROUP - CODE B | BILLING INFORMATION |
| RETURN LOCATION JNB AIRPORT | TOUR CODE No |
| REMARKS INCL: CDW/PAI/TLW/UM/TAX/SURCHARGE | |

**2** Claudio and Flavia had to pay more because they arranged a one-way rental. Read this part of the Terms and Conditions on the Avis South Africa website. How much more did they have to pay? Tick ✓ one of the boxes.

a ZAR 123.12 ☐
b ZAR 264.24 ☐
c ZAR 406.98 ☐
d ZAR 615.60 ☐

**3** Look again at the *Remarks* section of the rental voucher. How many extras have Claudio and Flavia paid for? Write a list.

**4** Claudio and Flavia look for explanations of these extras in this other part of the Terms and Conditions. Scan the webpage on the right and answer these questions.

a Which extras on the rental voucher are explained?

------------------------------------------------

b What do the abbreviations stand for?

------------------------------------------------
------------------------------------------------

c Can you guess the meaning of any abbreviations that are not explained?

------------------------------------------------

**5** Look at the Surcharges and Tax. Underline the charges that Claudio and Flavia have to pay.

**6** Claudio and Flavia have chosen Limited Cover accident insurance (CDW). If they have an accident, will they pay more or less than if they had chosen SCDW?

**7** Would you choose Limited Cover or Super Cover for accidents and theft? Why?

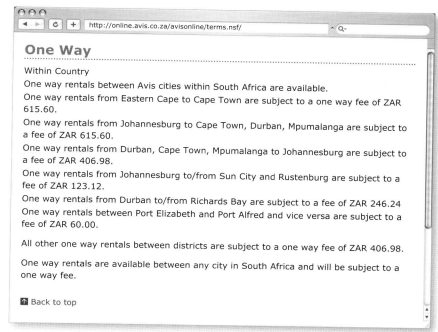

http://online.avis.co.za/avisonline/terms.nsf/

## One Way

Within Country

One way rentals between Avis cities within South Africa are available.

One way rentals from Eastern Cape to Cape Town are subject to a one way fee of ZAR 615.60.

One way rentals from Johannesburg to Cape Town, Durban, Mpumalanga are subject to a fee of ZAR 615.60.

One way rentals from Durban, Cape Town, Mpumalanga to Johannesburg are subject to a fee of ZAR 406.98.

One way rentals from Johannesburg to/from Sun City and Rustenburg are subject to a fee of ZAR 123.12.

One way rentals from Durban to/from Richards Bay are subject to a fee of ZAR 246.24

One way rentals between Port Elizabeth and Port Alfred and vice versa are subject to a fee of ZAR 60.00.

All other one way rentals between districts are subject to a one way fee of ZAR 406.98.

One way rentals are available between any city in South Africa and will be subject to a one way fee.

⬆ Back to top

ZAR = South African Rands

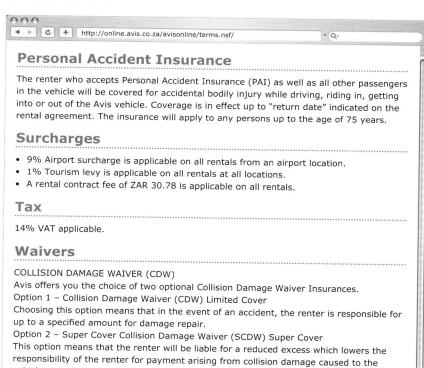

http://online.avis.co.za/avisonline/terms.nsf/

## Personal Accident Insurance

The renter who accepts Personal Accident Insurance (PAI) as well as all other passengers in the vehicle will be covered for accidental bodily injury while driving, riding in, getting into or out of the Avis vehicle. Coverage is in effect up to "return date" indicated on the rental agreement. The insurance will apply to any persons up to the age of 75 years.

## Surcharges

- 9% Airport surcharge is applicable on all rentals from an airport location.
- 1% Tourism levy is applicable on all rentals at all locations.
- A rental contract fee of ZAR 30.78 is applicable on all rentals.

## Tax

14% VAT applicable.

## Waivers

COLLISION DAMAGE WAIVER (CDW)
Avis offers you the choice of two optional Collision Damage Waiver Insurances.
Option 1 – Collision Damage Waiver (CDW) Limited Cover
Choosing this option means that in the event of an accident, the renter is responsible for up to a specified amount for damage repair.
Option 2 – Super Cover Collision Damage Waiver (SCDW) Super Cover
This option means that the renter will be liable for a reduced excess which lowers the responsibility of the renter for payment arising from collision damage caused to the vehicle or part thereof.
THEFT LOSS WAIVER
Avis offers you the choice of two optional Theft Loss Waiver Insurances.
Option 1 – Theft Loss Waiver (TLW) Limited Cover
Choosing this option means that in the event of theft of a vehicle or part thereof, the renter is responsible for up to a specified amount for the replacement of the applicable loss by theft. Personal property is not covered.
Option 2 – Super Theft Loss Waiver (STLW) Super Cover
This option means that the renter will be liable for a reduced excess which lowers the responsibility of the renter for payment arising from theft of a vehicle or part thereof. Personal property is not covered.

# B Safe driving in South Africa

1 Claudio and Flavia arrive in Cape Town and go to Avis to collect their car. The rental agent gives them the envelope on the right which contains the rental agreement. Should they keep the envelope until the end of their trip?

## Did you know ...?

In most countries, vehicles are driven on the right-hand side of the road. However, in some countries, such as Australia, India, Indonesia, Ireland, Japan, Malaysia, New Zealand, Thailand, the UK and South Africa, vehicles are driven on the left-hand side.

In most countries, speed and distances are measured in kilometres. In the UK and the USA, however, speed and distances are measured in miles. There are approximately 1.6 kilometres to the mile.

2 The agent tells Claudio and Flavia that they always need to carry cash when driving. Read the information on the envelope and find out why. Complete what the rental agent tells them.

> You'll need to carry cash because ..............................
> .......................................................
> .......................................................

---

KINDLY INDICATE YOUR RETURN KM READING, FUEL GAUGE READING, DATE AND TIME, AND RETURN THIS ENVELOPE, WITH YOUR KEYS, TO THE RENTAL COUNTER.

DOCUMENT NUMBER

| RETURN KM READING | | | | | | | | | |
|---|---|---|---|---|---|---|---|---|---|
| RETURN FUEL GAUGE ✓ | E | $1/8$ | $1/4$ | $3/8$ | $1/2$ | $5/8$ | $3/4$ | $7/8$ | F |

| RETURN DATE | RETURN TIME |
|---|---|

## Safe Driving in South Africa

**DRIVER'S LICENCE**
When driving, you must be in possession of your driver's licence at all times.

**SEAT BELTS**
The law requires that you wear seat belts at all times.

**DRIVING**
In South Africa, driving is on the left-hand side of the road.

**SPEED LIMITS**
Generally 60 km/hr in built-up areas, 100 km/hr in rural areas and 120 km/hr on highways.

**PETROL**
Petrol is available 24 hours per day. Unleaded petrol should be used in Avis cars. Credit cards are not accepted for the payment of petrol.

**SAFETY**
For your own safety, keep your doors locked while driving.

**LOCK UP**
Shut windows and lock all doors and the boot when leaving the vehicle unattended.

**VALUABLES**
Do not leave personal belongings such as cell phones and valuables in your vehicle. They are not covered by our insurance.

**TYRES**
Avis undertakes that on delivery of the vehicle to the renter, the condition of the tyres will be in compliance with legislation and the tyre pressure in accordance with the vehicle manufacturer's specification for 'normal use'.

It is the responsibility of the renter to ensure that both the condition and inflation of the tyres are appropriate throughout the course of the rental.

It is the responsibility of the renter to inspect the condition of the tyres at commencement of the rental and to make adjustments to the tyre pressure to take into account such factors as the number of passengers, mass of luggage, ambient temperatures, speed and road condition.

**IMMOBILISER**
Please use the immobiliser when leaving the vehicle unattended.

**ROAD MAPS**
Maps of Southern Africa, including city and regional maps, can be found in a copy of the Avis Inbound magazine, in each vehicle or at the Avis Customer Service Centre. More extensive area maps are obtainable from the Automobile Association (AA) and South African Tourism.

**Avis Careline: +27 (0)800 001 669**
**24 hour breakdown and medical emergencies**

Avis Central Reservations:
National: +27 (0)861 021 111
International: +27 (0)861 034 444
Preferred Service: +27 (0)861 113 333
Website: www.avis.co.za

Avis rents Volkswagen and other fine cars.

AVIS
We try harder.

**3** Claudio and Flavia don't want to break the law when they are driving in South Africa. What four things do they have to do to stay within the law? Complete what Flavia tells Claudio.

a   We have to carry our driving licences all the time.

b   We _____

c   We _____

d   We _____

**4** What four pieces of advice does the information on the envelope give? Complete what Claudio tells Flavia.

a   We should keep our doors locked while driving.

b   We _____

c   We _____

d   We _____

**5** Which part of the car should Claudio and Flavia check regularly?

_____

**6** Which telephone number on the envelope is probably the most useful for Claudio and Flavia while they are in South Africa? Why?

_____

**Focus on ...**
**vocabulary**

On the Avis rental agreement envelope there are some useful words about cars and driving. Find words on the envelope which match these definitions.
a   a closed space at the back of a car for storing things
    b o o t
b   something such as a car or bus that takes people from one place to another, especially using roads
    _ _ _ _ _ _ _ _
c   a thick, round piece of rubber filled with air, that fits around a wheel _ _ _ _
d   a device fitted to a car which stops it from moving so that it cannot be stolen _ _ _ _ _ _ _ _ _ _ _ _

Compound nouns are nouns which consist of two words. Find compound nouns on the envelope which match these definitions.
e   a piece of equipment that you use to measure how much petrol you have used _ _ _ _ _ _ _ _ _ _
f   an official document that allows you to drive a car
    _ _ _ _ _ _ _ _ _ _ _ _ _
g   a strap that you fasten across your body when travelling in a vehicle _ _ _ _ _ _ _ _
h   the fastest speed that a vehicle is allowed to travel on a particular road _ _ _ _ _ _ _ _ _ _
i   fuel that does not contain lead
    _ _ _ _ _ _ _ _ _ _ _ _ _

**Can-do checklist**

Tick what you can do.

| | Can do | Need more practice |
|---|---|---|
| I can search a text for abbreviations and particular words. | ✔ | ✔ |
| I can find out what car rental payments include. | | |
| I can understand driving laws and road safety advice. | | |

# Unit 3
# Somewhere to live

go to Useful language p. 83

## Get ready to read

- Circle the words in these sentences so that they are true for you.
  I live *on my own / with other people*.
  I live in a *flat / house*.
  I *own / rent* the property.
  I *share a room / have my own room*.

- How would you try to find accommodation if you moved to a different town or country? Tick ✓ the things you would do.
  I'd go to an accommodation agency. ☐
  I'd look in the newspaper. ☐
  I'd advertise in the newspaper. ☐
  I'd look on the Internet. ☐
  I'd advertise on the Internet. ☐
  I'd ask friends if they knew of any accommodation. ☐

## A Looking for a room

### Learning tip

The texts in this book are real texts written for ordinary people. These people read the texts with a purpose in mind – for example, people read accommodation advertisements like those in this unit because they want a place to live.
When you read a text, ask yourself: Who would read this text? Why would they read it? Understanding who would read something, and why, will help you to read the text as if you were reading it in the real world.

1 Imagine you are moving to a new town and want to rent a room. What do you need to know about a room before you see it? Look at the examples, and then write four more questions.

When is it available?
Is it near the town centre?
----------------------------------------
----------------------------------------
----------------------------------------
----------------------------------------

2 Look at these internet advertisements for accommodation in and around Cambridge. Can you find the answers to all your questions in each advertisement?

File  Edit  View  Favorites  Tools  Help

Address [                                    ] Go   Links »

a  Chesterton, double room for non-smoker in friendly mixed shared house, let from beginning February, £225 per calendar month excluding bills. Call 07967 920745.

----------------------------------------

b  Ground-floor single bedroom with own bathroom. Suit professional male. £85 per week including bills. Ten minutes from city centre on foot. Email: boxleyrooms@hotmail.co.uk

----------------------------------------

c  Available 8 January for eight months: two furnished rooms in fabulous new house near A14. All modern conveniences – double glazing, gas central heating, power shower, etc. Broadband, off-road parking. £455 per month all inclusive. References required. Phone 01223 34109 evenings.

----------------------------------------

d  Female wanted for a nice furnished room in a family home, £75 per week, all inclusive. Move in as soon as possible. Long or short term. Phone Carol 01223 73926.

3 Look at the newspaper advertisements on the right, which are also for accommodation in and around Cambridge. Why are they more difficult to understand than the internet advertisements?

4 Work out the meaning of the abbreviations in the newspaper advertisements. If you need some help, you will find all these words in the internet advertisements.

Advertisement e
sgl rm: __single room__   nr: _____   f n/s: _____
pcm all incl: _____   avail beg Jan: _____

Advertisement f
mins: _____   d/g + gas c/h: _____   ASAP: _____
mths: _____   Refs req.: _____

Advertisement g
1 bed: _____   furn: _____   prof couple: _____
mod cons: _____   pcm excl bills: _____   eves: _____

Advertisement h
dbl rm: _____   m owner: _____   pw incl bills: _____

e **Lovely**, sgl rm in shared house nr city centre, f n/s, £295 pcm all incl, avail beg Jan. Email: Jane6@virgin.net

f **Large** room, 2 mins railway station, d/g + gas c/h, let from ASAP for 6 mths. Refs req. 07822 867544

g **Wood Road**, 1 bed furn flat, suit prof couple, all mod cons. £500 pcm excl bills + deposit. Phone Gloria on 01223 43673 eves.

h **Sunny** dbl rm, house shared with m owner, garage, £70 pw incl bills. Phone Steve on 01223 56220.

5 Look again at advertisements a–h. Find the best accommodation for each of these people. Read the example before you begin.

**Ryuichi** is from Japan. He works as a translator for a company in the centre of Cambridge. When Ryuichi came to Britain, he started smoking again. __b__

The room in advertisement b is near the centre of town and is suitable for a professional male. Also, the advertisement doesn't ask for a non-smoker.

**Julia** is only in Cambridge for two months. She wants to live with a British family so that she can improve her English as much as possible. _____
**Marina** and **Stefan** have just got married. Marina has a job teaching German in a secondary school. They don't particularly want to share accommodation with other people. _____
**Pei Lan** is studying in Cambridge from the beginning of January until the end of June when she goes back home to Taiwan. Some of her friends are studying in London and she sometimes visits them there. _____
**Ibrahim** is from Qatar. He has a car, which he uses most weekends. His cousin is arriving in Cambridge very soon. He is going to study at the same language school as Ibrahim and also needs a room. _____
**Mirella** would like to share with women, preferably British ones. She doesn't smoke or drive and is happy to rent a small room. _____
**Tolga** works in a hotel outside Cambridge and he drives there every day. He now has a small room and would like something larger. _____
**Aleksy** doesn't want to pay more than £60 a week. He doesn't want to live on his own or with a family. He's a non-smoker. _____

6 Imagine you are going to study English in Cambridge and need somewhere to live. Would you be interested in any of the accommodation in advertisements a–h? Why? / Why not?

## Did you know …?

If you are looking for a room to rent in the UK, you will find advertisements in the local newspaper, in newsagents' and post office windows, and on the Internet. You may also be able to get a list of accommodation agencies from the local Tourist Information Office.

## Class bonus

Work in pairs and write an advertisement for a room. Use abbreviations where possible. Exchange your advertisements with other pairs of students. Find a room you would like to rent.

## E X tra practice

Look at rented accommodation in the UK at the website www.roomsforlet.co.uk Find a room you would like to rent.

# B Signing a contract

## Did you know …?

You usually have to sign a tenancy agreement before you move into a room, flat or house that you are going to rent. When you sign a tenancy agreement, you need a witness. This person watches you sign to confirm that your signature is genuine.

The language of these agreements can be old-fashioned and formal – even native English speakers have problems understanding it. However, a tenancy agreement is a legally binding contract so it is very important to understand what you are signing. If a tenant – the person who is renting the flat – breaks one of the conditions, the landlord – the owner – could take them to court.

**1 On pages 18 and 19 you looked at some advertisements and matched them with people looking for accommodation. Scan this tenancy agreement and answer these questions.**

a Which person from page 19 signed this agreement?

-----------------------------------

b Which property from page 18 or 19 is the agreement for?

-----------------------------------

c Who witnessed the tenant's signature?

-----------------------------------

d What do we know about the tenant's witness?

-----------------------------------

# TENANCY AGREEMENT

## DEFINITIONS

THE LANDLORD Mrs Gloria Black of 6 Sutton Road, Cambridge CB5 7AQ
THE TENANT Marina Kahn
PROPERTY 24a Wood Road, Cambridge CB2 8BG
TOGETHER WITH CONTENTS (fixtures, furniture and equipment) specified in the inventory (attached)
TERM from 1st January 20__ to 31st December 20__ (12 months)
RENT £500 per calendar month, payable in advance on the first day of each month
DEPOSIT £500, payable on commencement of this Agreement

## AGREEMENTS

A  The Landlord may re-enter the Property and terminate this Agreement if the Rent or any part of it is not paid within fourteen days after it becomes due.
B  The Landlord may bring the tenancy to an end at any time before the expiry of the Term (but not earlier than six months from the Commencement Date of this Contract) by giving the Tenant not less than two months' written notice stating that the Landlord requires possession of the Property.
C  The Landlord shall put the deposit with The Deposit Protection Service, and shall inform the Tenant within 14 days of taking the deposit of the contact details of this service and details of how to apply for the release of the deposit from this service.

## TENANT'S OBLIGATIONS

1  Pay the Rent into the Landlord's bank account at the times specified; and pay interest of 15 per cent per annum on any rent which is more than 14 days overdue.
2  Pay for all water, gas and electricity consumed on the Property during the Term; and pay in full for all charges made for the use of the telephone on the Property during the Term; and pay in full any council tax liable on the Property.
3  Keep the interior of the Property during the Term in a good and clean state of repair, condition and decoration; and make good all damage and breakages to the Property and its contents which may occur during the Term.
4  Permit the Landlord to enter the Property at all reasonable times: to inspect the Property and its contents; and to carry out any works of maintenance or repair to the Property which the Landlord may consider to be necessary; to show prospective new Tenants around the Property at the end of the tenancy.
5  Not take in any paying guest without the prior written consent of the Landlord.
6  Not use the Property other than as a private dwelling; nor carry on any profession, trade or business in the Property.
7  Not use any musical instrument, wireless or television between midnight and 7 am, nor permit any singing or dancing between these hours.
8  Not fix a wireless or television aerial to the exterior of the Property; nor fix any notice, sign, advertisement or poster to the exterior or windows of the Property.
9  Not keep in the Property any cat, dog or other pet without the prior written consent of the Landlord.
10  Deliver up the Property to the Landlord at the end of the tenancy in the same good and clean state of repair, condition and decoration as it was in at the commencement of the Term (fair wear and tear, and damage by accidental fire excepted).

## SIGNATURES

Tenant:        Name (print): _MARINA KAHN_        Signed: _Marina Kahn_
Witnessed by: Name (print): _ALICE RACE_        Signed: _A. Race_
                    Occupation: _Secondary school teacher_
                    Address: _16 School House Lane, Cambridge, CB2 8GH_

Landlord:    Name (print): _GLORIA BLACK_        Signed: _Gloria Black_
Witnessed by: Name (print): _OLIVE LYDIA LEE_        Signed: _Olive L Lee_
                    Occupation: _Librarian_
                    Address: _3 Fieldhead Road, Peterborough PB4 8DU_

**2** Marina asks Alice to explain the agreement. Look at the *Definitions* and *Agreements* sections. Then (circle) the correct words in Alice's explanations.

a The tenancy starts on 1 January and lasts for *six /* (*twelve*) months.
b If you don't pay your March rent before *1 March / 15 March*, Gloria can ask you to leave the property.
c If Gloria needs the flat, she must write to you *two / three* months before she wants you to leave.
d Gloria *will / won't* keep your deposit in her bank account.
e She *must / needn't* tell you how to get your deposit back.

**3** Look at the *Tenant's Obligations* section. Match Alice's explanations a–j with points 1–10.

a You can't listen to music during the night. ...... *point 7* ......
b You can't put anything on the outside wall of the flat. ----------------------
c You have to pay the rent on the first day every month. ----------------------
d You have to let Gloria into the flat if she wants to look at it. ----------------------
e When you leave the flat, the flat must be as clean as it is now. ----------------------
f You have to pay all your bills. ----------------------
g You must get Gloria's permission in writing if you want a friend to stay and pay part of the rent. ----------------------
h You can't set up a business in the flat. ----------------------
i You must get Gloria's permission in writing before you get a pet. ----------------------
j You have to look after the flat properly. ----------------------

**4** Answer Marina's questions with *yes* or *no*. <u>Underline</u> the information in the agreement which gives the answer.

a Do we have to pay council tax? ...*yes*...
b If we pay the rent more than 14 days late, do we have to pay interest?
c Can we have all-night parties?
d Do we have to pay for the telephone?
e Can Gloria show new tenants around the flat while we're still here?
f Can we put notices in the windows?

---

**Focus on ...**
**formal language**

There are many formal words and phrases in this tenancy agreement. For example, *terminate*, means 'to end' and *becomes due* means 'is owed' in Agreement A.

Find these phrases in the tenancy agreement, and (circle) the correct informal equivalent of the word(s) in *italics*.

a the *expiry* of the Term — beginning / (*end*)
b the *Commencement* Date — beginning / end
c written *notice* — advice / warning
d *inform* the tenant — ask / tell
e water, gas and electricity *consumed* — used / provided
f prior written *consent* — agreement / arrangement
g the *exterior* of the Property — top / outside

---

**Can-do checklist**

Tick what you can do.

| | Can do | Need more practice |
|---|---|---|
| I can put myself in the position of someone reading advertisements in the real world. | ✔ | ✔ |
| I can understand advertisements for rented accommodation. | | |
| I can work out the meaning of abbreviations. | | |
| I can understand a tenancy agreement. | | |

# Unit 4
# I'll check it in

go to Useful language p. 83

**Get ready to** read

- Look at the luggage in the picture and circle the correct words.
  a rucksack / vanity case
  b garment bag / suitcase
  c briefcase / holdall
  d suitcase / vanity case
  e garment bag / holdall
  f briefcase / rucksack

- Which of these items of luggage do you usually travel with?

## A How much luggage have you got?

1 Miklós is going to fly from Paris to Toronto on an Air Canada flight. He knows he can take one bag as hand luggage (or 'carry-on baggage'). However, he doesn't know how much luggage he can check in, so he looks on the Air Canada website. Skim this webpage. Is it the one he needs?

**Learning tip**

We usually look at a text quickly to find out what it is about. This type of reading is called skimming. When we skim, we get the main idea and don't pay attention to the small details. Skimming is very often the first step in reading a text.

### AIR CANADA 🍁
#### Checked Baggage Allowances

Customers are allowed to check the following amounts of luggage free of charge:

| | Maximum number of bags (per person) | Maximum weight per bag | Maximum linear dimensions per bag (length + height + width) |
|---|---|---|---|
| Economy Class | 2 bags | 23 kg (50 lb) | 158 cm (62 in) |
| Executive Class, Executive First and Star Alliance Gold | 3 bags | 32 kg (70 lb) Total weight of all 3 bags not to exceed 69 kg (150 lb) | 158 cm (62 in) |
| Air Canada Elite and Super Elite (in any class of service) | 4 bags | 32 kg (70 lb) Total weight of all 4 bags not to exceed 92 kg (200 lb) | 158 cm (62 in) |

lb = pound    kg = kilogram    in = inch    cm = centimetres

2 Does the webpage give the information in a–d below? Skim the webpage again and tick ✓ one or more of the boxes.

a the size of the luggage passengers can check in ☐
b the weight of the luggage passengers can check in ☐
c the number of items of luggage passengers can check in ☐
d the cost of checking in excess baggage ☐

3 Miklós is planning to travel Economy Class. Find out the following.

a the largest size suitcase he can check in

b the total weight of luggage he can check in

4 Miklós wants to check in more luggage than his free allowance, so he looks at the Excess Baggage Fees webpage. Skim the webpage and find three situations when you have to pay an excess baggage fee to Air Canada.

## AIR CANADA ✿

### Excess Baggage Fees

When travelling on Air Canada, the size and number of bags you check is limited by the free checked baggage allowance. If your baggage exceeds this free allowance (too many pieces, too big or too heavy), you will be charged an excess baggage fee.

Excess baggage is accepted subject to space availability. Currency exchange may affect amount to be paid. Applicable taxes are not included in the prices.

**Note:** Please arrive at the airport at least 60 min before departure if checking overweight or oversized baggage. More than one excess fee may be applied. For example, if the item is overweight and oversize, it will be charged twice.

For oversized (more than 115 in / 292 cm) or overweight bags (more than 70 lb / 32 kg), please contact your Air Canada Cargo Local Sales Office for handling.

**Economy Class**

| Type of excess | Restriction | Excess Fee<br>More than one excess fee may be applied. |
|---|---|---|
| Overweight | Between 23 kg and 32 kg (50 lb–70 lb) | $35 CAD ($30 USD) per bag |
| Oversized* | Between 160 cm and 292 cm (63 in–115 in) | $35 CAD ($30 USD) per bag |
| Extra baggage<br>More than 2 bags | North America (Canada/US/Mexico) | $105 CAD ($91 USD) per bag |
| | International (all other destinations) ** | $175 CAD ($152 USD) per bag |

\* Sizes indicate linear dimensions per bag (length + width + depth)
\*\* Excludes Brazil and Japan (Please contact Air Canada Reservations for details on excess fees to these destinations)

5 Miklós wants to check in this luggage. What excess baggage fee will he have to pay? Tick ✓ one of the boxes.

$35 CAD ☐   $70 CAD ☐   $105 CAD ☐

6 Other Economy Class passengers on Miklós's flight want to check in the following items of luggage. Will each passenger have to pay an excess baggage fee? Write Y (yes) or N (no).

a two medium-sized suitcases – one weighing 22 kg and the other weighing 30 kg  Y
b two large suitcases – each measuring more than 160 cm, but weighing less than 23 kg  ......
c two medium-sized suitcases – all within the weight and size restrictions  ......
d one suitcase weighing 22 kg, with the following dimensions: 80 x 40 x 30 cm  ......

7 Have you ever paid an excess baggage fee? How much did you have to pay?

### Focus on ...
**the prefix over**

A prefix is a group of letters which you add to the beginning of one word to make another.

Complete these sentences with over and the words from the list.

crowded  ~~done~~  due  grown  priced  rated

a If vegetables are cooked too long, they are _overdone_.
b If a garden is full of plants that have become too big, it is ......... .
c If you forget to take your book back to the library, it is ......... .
d If there are too many people in a place, it is ......... .
e If a film is considered to be better than it really is, it is ......... .
f If something is too expensive, it is ......... .

### Class bonus

Think of five items you cannot travel without. Compare your list with someone else's. Are any of your items the same?

## B Where's my luggage?

1 Miklós flies from Paris Charles de Gaulle Airport to Lester B Pearson International Airport in Toronto. Unfortunately, when he goes to Baggage Reclaim his holdall and suitcase do not appear. What do you think he should do? Write your answer.

I think ................................................................................

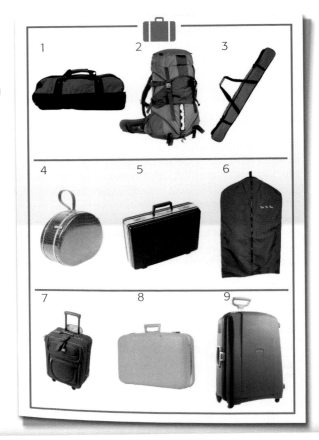

2 Miklós goes to the lost luggage desk to ask for help and is shown a card which illustrates different types of luggage. Look at the pictures on the card and match them with the descriptions below. Write the number in the boxes.

a medium hardshell suitcase ☒8
b briefcase ☐
c large rucksack ☐
d ski bag ☐
e small soft-sided trolley suitcase ☐
f extra-large holdall ☐
g large hardshell trolley suitcase ☐
h garment bag ☐
i vanity case ☐

3 Miklós is given this form to fill in. Read the introduction. Should he be optimistic about getting his luggage back soon?

## Missing items

Dear Customer

We are sorry that your baggage was mishandled during your recent flight and would be grateful if you could complete the form below to assist us in tracing it.

We would like to assure you that every effort will be made to locate your baggage and return it to you as soon as possible. We are pleased to report that the vast majority of delayed bags are found and returned to their owners within 48 hours.

If your baggage has not been located within 48 hours, we will continue to trace it for a maximum of three months.

PLEASE WRITE CLEARLY USING BLOCK CAPITALS

NAME: ........................................................................................

ADDRESS AT DESTINATION: ........................................................

TELEPHONE/MOBILE NUMBER: ...................................................

DATE OF TRAVEL: .......................................................................

FROM: ...........................................  TO: ..............................................

FLIGHT NUMBER: ................................  BAGGAGE CHECK NUMBER: ..............................

| TYPE OF ITEM | SIZE | COLOUR |
| --- | --- | --- |
| | | |
| | | |
| | | |

Signature ........................................  Date ........................................

4 Use the information from Miklós's boarding card, the label on his rucksack and his baggage check label to fill in the missing items form. Remember to include information about his checked baggage in the picture on the right.

ECONOMY CLASS
name
MIKLÓS PILZINSKY
Class | Classe

Boarding time
Heure d'embarquement ▶

departure airport          To | Destination
PARIS CDG
flight                  time
AIR CANADA 854    13.30
Boarding Pass | Carte d'accès à bord

seat
        33B
date
    26th NOV

NAME Miklós Pilzinsky
DESTINATION ADDRESS 12-111
Carlton Tower Road, Toronto,
Ontario M4C 5L6
TELEPHONE (001) 416 333 4276
DESTINATION AIRPORT Toronto,
Lester B Pearson International

AIR CANADA
PILZINSKY
CDG      26NOV      13.30
TO: TORONTO
AC  854
0014    AC790278

## Did you know …?

Charles de Gaulle (1890–1970) was a French general who was the first President of the Fifth Republic (1959–1969).

Lester Bowles Pearson (1897–1970) was a senior advisor to the UN, President of the UN General Assembly (1952–3) and Canadian Prime Minister. He won the Nobel Peace Prize in 1957.

## E X tra practice

What should Miklós do if he doesn't get his luggage back? Look at the website www.aircanada.com Does it have any information about delayed baggage?

## Can-do checklist

Tick what you can do.

| | Can do | Need more practice |
|---|---|---|
| I can skim a webpage to get a general idea of what it is about. | | |
| I can find out how much checked baggage I can take on a plane. | | |
| I can fill in a form about delayed luggage. | | |

# Unit 5
# I'll be at home

## Get ready to read

- Which of these items of mail do you often receive? Tick ✓ one or more of the boxes.
  personal letters ☐  postcards ☐  official letters ☐  bills ☐
  goods you ordered ☐  junk mail ☐  perishable goods like food, flowers ☐

- Think about postal services in your country and decide if the following sentences are true (T) or false (F) for you.
  My mail is delivered through the letterbox in my front door. ......
  I collect my mail from a PO Box at my local post office. ......
  I sometimes have to sign for letters or parcels. ......
  I sometime have to collect letters or parcels from the post office. ......
  If I want to send something very quickly, I have to pay extra for special delivery. ......

go to Useful language p. 83

## A Sorry, you were out

1 **It is one o'clock on Monday 23 March. Raquel Ramos García has just come home to find this card with her mail. Scan it and complete the sentences.**

  a  The card is from .................................................................
  b  The card is for ...................................................................
  c  The card has been put through Raquel's door because
     .........................................................................................

2 **Look at the back of the card below. What would be a good heading for this side of the card? Tick ✓ one of the boxes.**

  a  We'll call again ☐
  b  How to get your item ☐
  c  Royal Mail Services in your area ☐

---

**Royal Mail**

### Sorry, you were out

| Time 12.32 | Today's date 23 March |
|---|---|

Name  Raquel Ramos García
Address  133 Charlton Road
         Reading        Postcode RG24 7AW

**You were out and your**
☐ Special Delivery      ☐ Letter    ☐ International item
☑ Recorded Signed For   ☐ Packet    ☐ Perishable item
**could not be delivered to you**         ☐ Large item

**because**
☑ A signature is required
☐ It's too big for your letterbox
**Please see overleaf for information on where your item is now.**

Item number  ZH 5631 8734 5GB
Delivery person duty number

www.royalmail.com/redelivery

---

**Your item has been left:**
☐ In your 'Safeplace' on your property at:
☐ with your designated neighbour at:

☑ **Has been returned to the Royal Mail Delivery Office at:**

Royal Mail
Reading Delivery Office
84 Caversham Road
Reading,
Berkshire, RG1 1AA        TEL: 08456 113 227
**HOURS:  MON-FRI:  0600 - 1800**
         **SAT:      0600 - 1230**

**You can:**
**Collect the item.** Please leave ⌐2⌐ hours before collecting. You'll need to bring evidence of your identity such as a passport or bank card. If someone's collecting on your behalf, they'll need to provide proof of your identity.

**Redelivery or "Local Collect" services:**
to arrange visit us online at **www.royalmail.com/redelivery** or call the number above.
We can **Redeliver** to your address or to an alternative local address (unfortunately, we can't redeliver Special Delivery items to an alternative address).
Or for 50p you can have your item taken to a local Post Office® Branch for you to pick up using our **"Local Collect"** service.

Please note we'll keep a Recorded item for 1 week, and all other items for 3 weeks before returning them to the sender.

---

## Did you know …?

Reading is a large town on the River Thames between London and Oxford. The pronunciation of Reading, the city, is /redɪŋ/. (What you are doing with this book is /riːdɪŋ/.) Note also that the pronunciation of the administrative region – or county – Berkshire is /baːkʃə/.

## Learning tip

We often skim a text the first time we read it – we read it quickly to get a general sense. Alternatively, we scan a text – we read it quickly to find a particular piece of information. After a quick read, we sometimes go back and read parts of the text more carefully to find out further, more detailed information. We can use any combination of these different reading skills to find the information we need.

**3** Scan the front and back of the card on the opposite page and choose the correct ending for these sentences. Tick ✓ one of the boxes.

a  Raquel's item of mail is
   in the shed in the garden. ☐
   with a neighbour. ☐
   going back to the Delivery Office. ☐
b  The earliest she can collect the item is
   2.00 pm. ☐
   2.32 pm. ☐
   two hours after finding the card. ☐

**4** Raquel asks a neighbour to explain how to get her item of mail. Read the back of the card again and decide if what the neighbour says is true (T) or false (F). Correct the information that is wrong.

a  If you go and collect the letter yourself, you have to prove that you're the person it's addressed to. _T_
b  If someone else goes for you, they have to show their passport or bank card. _____
c  You have to phone if you want to collect the letter. _____
d  They charge extra if you have the letter delivered to someone else's house. _____
e  You have to pay if you want to collect the letter from your nearest post office. _____
f  You have four weeks from when you get the card to collect your letter. _____

**5** Raquel wants her mail to be redelivered to a friend's house on Wednesday. She goes to www.royalmail.com/redelivery to arrange this. Read the webpage below and decide which friend Raquel's mail should be redelivered to.

a  Claudia Santos, 3 Harris Gardens, Reading RG17 3PE ☐
b  Sam Williams, 15 St Mary's Way, Reading RG24 6TR ☐
c  Aisha Hussein, Flat 2, 26 Water Lane, Reading RG12 1RR ☐

It's easy to arrange Redelivery. Just select "Arrange redelivery now" to find out more.

### Redeliver to your own address

We can redeliver your item to your address on a day that is convenient to you, free of charge.

### Redeliver to a different address

With the exception of Special Delivery services, we can deliver your item to a different address within the same postcode area, e.g. a neighbour's house, free of charge.  A postcode area is determined by your local Delivery Office, and is the area that they deliver to.  We cannot redeliver to an address outside of this area.  In most cases, for example, if you live in SE25 the same postcode area would be any other postcode starting with SE25.

## Class bonus

Raquel decides to have the item delivered to her friend's house on Wednesday. Why does she choose this option, do you think? Why doesn't she choose any of the other options? How many reasons can you suggest?
Work with a partner and discuss your answers. Have you got any different reasons?

# B Run the cold tap

**1** Raquel also finds a leaflet with her mail. Scan the back of the leaflet on the right and find the answers to these questions.

a Who is the leaflet from?

--------------------------------------------------

b Who is it for?

--------------------------------------------------

c Why has it been put through the door?

--------------------------------------------------

**2** Skim the inside of the leaflet below. Which of these things does this part of the leaflet do? Tick ✓ one or more of the boxes.

a explains in general terms why the water has to be turned off ☐
b explains exactly why the water has to be turned off on Saturday ☐
c gives advice about what to do while the water is turned off ☐
d gives advice about what to do when the water is turned on again ☐

Thames Water

# interruptions
to your **water** supply

**Warning** of essential work in your area

**This is notice of essential work in your area that will interrupt your water supply**

We will have to turn off your water supply for

........2........ hours on ..28 March......

If the water is turned off for more than 6 hours, you can get water from

..................................................

The table below shows when the interruptions to your water supply are likely to start

|           | Morning | Afternoon |
|-----------|---------|-----------|
| Monday    |         |           |
| Tuesday   |         |           |
| Wednesday |         |           |
| Thursday  |         |           |
| Friday    |         |           |
| Saturday  | X       |           |
| Sunday    |         |           |

# Why we need to interrupt your water supply

We supply drinking water to over seven million customers through nearly 31,000 km of pipes. We are spending £1 million a day to ensure this service is provided, because these pipes sometimes need attention. In order to do this, we have to cut off your water supply from time to time because of planned or urgent work.

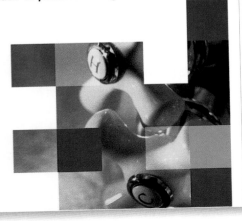

# For your guidance

**Do not use any household appliances that would normally use water, including a washing machine or dishwasher, while the water is off.**

Switch your central heating system off.

**Once the water supply returns**

Please run the cold tap nearest to the inlet pipe, which is normally in the kitchen.

Allow at least 2–5 minutes until the water runs clear.

**If your water does not come back on then please:**

• Check with a neighbour to see if their supply has been restored
• Check that the inside stop valve* is fully open by turning it off and turning it on again

**If this does not solve the problem**

Please call us on **0845 9200 800** (all calls are charged at local rates)

**Thank you for your co-operation.**

*A valve is a device which opens and closes to control the flow of liquids or gases.

**3** Raquel is going to be at home on Saturday, 28 March. Which of these things can she do that morning? (Circle) *can* or *can't* so that the sentences are correct.

a She (can) / *can't* use the vacuum cleaner.
b She *can* / *can't* do her washing.
c She *can* / *can't* have the central heating on.
d She *can* / *can't* flush the toilet.
e She *can* / *can't* use the microwave.

**4** It is now Sunday. This is what happened on Saturday afternoon. Read the inside of the leaflet again to help you put the events in the correct order.

a The Thames Water representative told her the water would be reconnected by five o'clock. ☐
b She tried the tap again at two o'clock in the afternoon, and there was still no water. 2
c The neighbour said that her water had come back on at half past twelve. ☐
d Raquel tried the tap at midday Saturday, but there was no water. 1
e She turned on the cold tap in the kitchen and let it run for five minutes. ☐
f She asked her neighbour if her water had come back on. ☐
g She called 0845 9200 800 because she still didn't have any water. ☐
h Two hours later Raquel was in the bathroom when she discovered that the water was back on. ☐
i Raquel checked the stop valve and it seemed to be fully open. ☐
j Then she had her shower. ☐

**Can-do checklist**

Tick what you can do.

| | Can do | Need more practice |
|---|---|---|
| I can use a variety of skills when reading texts. | | |
| I can follow instructions about having my mail redelivered. | | |
| I can follow instructions about having my water supply interrupted. | | |

# Unit 6
# A weekend in Wales

## Get ready to read

- Label the countries of the United Kingdom with the names in the box.

  | England   Northern Ireland   Scotland   Wales |

a _____

d _____

c _____

b _____

- How much do you know about Wales? Which of these sentences do you think are true? Tick ✓ one or more of the boxes.
  - a The national sport of Wales is golf. ☐
  - b Some people speak Welsh as their first language. ☐
  - c Wales is a wonderful holiday destination for people who like walking, climbing and other outdoor pursuits. ☐
  - d Wales has three national parks which include beautiful mountains and coastal areas. ☐

go to Useful language p. 83

## A Find your Welsh holiday here

**1 Sebastian is asking his friend Geraint about places to visit in Wales. Look at what Geraint says. Is he recommending St David's, or is he advising Sebastian not to go there?**

### Learning tip

Think about what you already know about a topic before you read a text about it. This allows you to relate what you read to what you already know, and it makes the new text easier to understand.

> St David's is like a village, but it's called a city because it's got a cathedral.

> The coast's beautiful around there — and if you get good weather, it's wonderful walking along the Coast Path.

> We went to an island where there were loads of birds — and no people.

> You can go surfing near St David's — the beaches and waves are wonderful, but the water's freezing!

**2 Sebastian decides to visit St David's, so he looks for some accommodation on the Internet. He finds the webpage opposite about a bed and breakfast. What extra information is there on it about the things Geraint mentioned? Read the webpage and complete the sentences.**

- a St David's is _the smallest city in Europe._
- b On the Coast Path _____
- c The beaches _____
- d There are birds _____

### Did you know …?

The population of Wales is about three million (5% of the UK population) and its capital is Cardiff. With its mountainous landscape and numerous sandy beaches, Wales has always attracted a lot of tourists. In 2002, for example, nearly 13 million trips of one night or more were made in Wales, generating expenditure of £1.8 billion. 11.9 million of these trips were made by UK residents.

**Bed & Breakfast – St David's**

## Ramsey House

Catering exclusively for adults, Ramsey House offers you professional hotel standards of accommodation and food service coupled with the friendly, relaxed atmosphere of a high-class non-smoking guest house.

Situated within walking distance of St David's, the smallest city in Europe, the house stands in its own attractive gardens and has private off-road parking. In the opposite direction, there is easy access to the Pembrokeshire Coast Path, where you can see some of Britain's most spectacular coastal scenery with its abundant bird life and wild flowers.

We have three double and three twin rooms. Each is individually furnished and decorated to 4-star standard with comfortable beds, central heating, remote control colour TV, hospitality trays, hair dryers and plenty of mirrors. All the rooms have a modern, well-lit en-suite bathroom with WC, shaver socket and electric shower.

All first-floor rooms have views of either the sea, the Cathedral or open country, and there are three ground-floor rooms with garden views, ideal for guests unable to climb stairs.

Our full Welsh breakfast offers you a great start to the day with homemade bread, muffins, marmalade and preserves. We can also prepare fresh picnic lunches for your day out walking the Coast Path or on the beaches.

There is a comfortable lounge with lots of books and leaflets about Pembrokeshire to help you plan your excursions. Weather permitting, guests may enjoy the peace and tranquillity of our gardens and watch the birds feeding. Drinks are served in both the garden and lounge.

We also have secure bicycle storage, a drying room and light laundry facilities.

Nearby are some of the safest and cleanest beaches in Europe offering a variety of water sports including sailing, surfing, wind-surfing and sea angling. Visitors are welcome at St David's City Golf Club and several other Pembrokeshire clubs. We are also conveniently situated for easy access to the bird sanctuary islands of Ramsey, Skomer and Skokholm.

A warm welcome awaits you at Ramsey House all year round. You will find it the ideal touring centre in all seasons.

Proprietors: Ceri & Elaine Morgan
01437 72021

**3** **Three of Sebastian's friends want to come to Wales with him. He writes an email to them about the accommodation. Complete his email.**

**From:** Sebastian
**Subject:** B&B in Wales

Hi everyone,
I've found a <sup>a</sup>_bed and breakfast_ on the Internet. It's called <sup>b</sup>_____ , and it's in a great location between <sup>c</sup>_____ and the Pembrokeshire Coast Path. If we want to do some walking, it sounds a good place to stay because they provide <sup>d</sup>_____ (should save on lunch bills). Also, there's a <sup>e</sup>_____ which will be useful if we get soaking wet walking in the rain. Oh, and the rooms are all <sup>f</sup>_____ , so we won't all have to share one bathroom! (Pete, you won't have to miss _Match of the Day_ because there's a TV in <sup>g</sup>_____ .) We can also take our bikes as there's <sup>h</sup>_____ .
What do you think?
Seb

**4** **Read these profiles of different tourists. Do you think they would like to stay at Ramsey House? Write _Y_ (yes) or _N_ (no) and <u>underline</u> the parts of the webpage which help you decide.**

a  Ana is a wheelchair user who enjoys holidays by the coast. __Y__
('ideal for guests unable to climb stairs')
b  Daniel wants to stay in St David's. _____
c  Sofia and Takis have just bought an expensive car and need safe parking. _____
d  Tina and Xavier are a married couple with two young children. _____

**5** **If you were going to Wales, would you like to stay at Ramsey House? Why? / Why not?**

E<u>X</u>tra practice

Choose one of the places in the webpage (for example, St David's, the Pembrokeshire Coast Path, Skomer) and find out five more facts about it on the Internet or from books.

## B Your room will be ready for you

**1** Sebastian makes some notes about the accommodation he and his friends want. He then phones Ramsey House. Read his notes and write the questions he asks in his phone conversation.

a  Have you got any rooms for four nights from 29 May?
b  ............................................................
c  ............................................................
d  ............................................................
e  ............................................................
f  ............................................................

*Notepad:*
tel: 01437 72021 MORGAN
4 nights: 29 May – 1 June incl?
4 people: 2 twin rooms?
Price?
Rooms available – what time?
Credit card?
Time we have to leave?

**2** Sebastian received this letter on 20 May. Who is it from?

............................................................

**3** Read the letter and find out if Sebastian can have the accommodation he wants. Write an answer for each of your questions in Exercise 1.

a  No, there are only rooms for three nights.
b  ............................................................
c  ............................................................
d  ............................................................
e  ............................................................
f  ............................................................

**4** Answer these questions about the cost of the accommodation.

a  How much has Sebastian already paid for the accommodation?
£140

b  How did he pay this?
............................................................

c  How much more will Sebastian and his friends have to pay at the end of their stay?
............................................................

d  How can they pay this?
............................................................

*Ramsey House*
*Lower Moor*
*St David's*
*Haverfordwest*
*Pembrokeshire SA62 6RP*

*Telephone: 01437 72021*

*Licensed Guest House*

18 May 20__

Mr Sebastian Rose
Flat 1
7 Cartwright Street
Edinburgh
EH18 8E2

Dear Mr Rose

Thank you for your deposit cheque for £140. We have pleasure in reserving the following accommodation for you:

ROOM/S: **2 twin en-suite rooms**
DATES: **Saturday, 29 May – Monday, 31 May (3 nights)**
DEPARTING AFTER BREAKFAST: **Tuesday, June 1st**

Our tariff is £35 per person per night for bed and breakfast.

Please note we do not operate a credit card facility. You are welcome to settle your account by cheque or cash.

When you book your holiday you are entering into a legally binding contract. Should you cancel this reservation for any reason within 4 weeks of arrival, and we are unable to re-let the accommodation, you will be liable for a cancellation charge up to the total cost of your holiday. You may, therefore, wish to insure your holiday against cancellation when arranging your general travel insurance. No allowance is made for meals not taken.

Your room will be ready for you from 2.00 pm on your day of arrival when we will do all we can to ensure the enjoyment of your visit.

Yours sincerely,

*Ceri Morgan*

Ceri and Elaine Morgan

**5** Which of these things does Ceri Morgan do in his letter? Tick ✓ one or more of the boxes and <u>underline</u> the parts of the letter where Ceri does these things.

a He thanks Sebastian for his phone call. ☐
b He cancels the reservation made over the phone. ☐
c He confirms Sebastian's reservation. ☐
d He explains the rules about cancelled reservations. ☐
e He advises Sebastian to arrange cancellation insurance. ☐
f He gives directions to Ramsey House. ☐

**6** Unfortunately, Sebastian's friends are ill the week after he receives the letter, so he decides to cancel the holiday. He reads the letter again before he phones Ramsey House. Answer these questions.

a What might happen to the money Sebastian has already paid?

----------------------------------------

b Might Sebastian and his friends have to pay the rest of their bill?

----------------------------------------

c In what circumstances would they get their money back?

----------------------------------------

d Would it make a difference if Sebastian had holiday insurance?

----------------------------------------

**7** Do you think the Morgans will manage to re-let the rooms Sebastian booked? Why? / Why not?

---

## Focus on ...
*should*

In his letter, Ceri Morgan writes 'Should you cancel this reservation … you will be liable for a cancellation charge'. We sometimes use *should* instead of *if* in formal written English.

Complete these sentences with *should* and a verb from the list.

| be change ~~damage~~ leave |
| require ring see worsen |

a ...<u>Should</u>... you ...<u>damage</u>... anything, you will be charged for it.
b -------------------- you -------------------- anyone in danger, you should call the coastguard.
c -------------------- we -------------------- out, you can collect the keys from next door.
d -------------------- you -------------------- anything behind, we will send it to you.
e -------------------- you -------------------- your mind, please return the goods within ten days.
f -------------------- the telephone -------------------- , please ignore it.
g -------------------- you -------------------- refreshments, we will be happy to provide tea and coffee.
h -------------------- the weather -------------------- , the trip will be cancelled.

---

## Class bonus

Work in pairs. One person is Sebastian and the other is Ceri Morgan. Act out the conversation between them when Sebastian phones to cancel his reservation.
Sebastian: Explain why you have to cancel.
Ceri: Explain the cancellation rules.

---

## Can-do checklist

Tick what you can do.

| | Can do | Need more practice |
|---|---|---|
| I can relate information I already know to what I read in a text. | ✓ | ✓ |
| I can understand a description of bed and breakfast accommodation. | | |
| I can understand a letter of confirmation and the rules about cancelled accommodation. | | |

# Unit 7
# I saw an article about it

## Get ready to read

- Do you ever read magazines? Tick ✓ the magazines you read.
  business and/or current affairs magazines ☐      computer magazines ☐
  sports magazines ☐                              magazines about celebrities ☐
  cookery magazines ☐                             fashion and/or photography magazines ☐
  holiday and/or travel magazines ☐               car and/or bike magazines ☐

- When do you usually buy magazines? How many do you buy a month? Do you keep them?

go to Useful language p. 84

## A Call of the wild

**1** Look at the article on the opposite page. What kind of magazine is it from?

_____

**2** What can you see in the photograph? What kind of animal is it?

_____

### Did you know ...?

The word *safari* comes from Swahili and Arabic. The Arabic word is *safar* meaning 'travel' or 'journey'. Swahili is one of the major languages of Kenya, Tanzania and Uganda.

Lots of words which are used in English have come from other languages. For example: *typhoon* (Chinese), *robot* (Czech), *cruise* (Dutch), *opera* (Italian), *judo* (Japanese), *ski* (Norwegian), *sofa* (Persian), *buffalo* (Portuguese), *yoghurt* (Turkish).

**3** Match these headings with the paragraphs in the article. Write each paragraph number in the correct box.
- a  Lodge or camp? ☐
- b  Where to go? ☐
- c  Drive, walk or boat? ☐
- d  What about other activities? ☐
- e  When to go? ☐1☐

**4** Read paragraph 1. Do these sentences describe the dry season (D) or the wet season (W)?
- a  There are more animals at each waterhole.  _D_
- b  There are more leaves on the trees and bushes.  _____
- c  You can't drive along some tracks.  _____
- d  There are fewer places to stay.  _____
- e  The animals can be seen more clearly.  _____
- f  Baby animals are born during this season.  _____

**5** Paragraphs 2 and 3 contrast several things. Read the paragraphs and think about the advantages of each situation below. Complete the sentences in your own words.
- a  If you camp, _you are always in the bush and you are very close to the animals._
- b  If you stay in a lodge, _____
- c  If you go on a game drive, _____
- d  If you go on a walking safari, _____
- e  If you go on a boat, _____

**6** Paragraphs 4 and 5 give several examples of travel destinations. Which region or country would you go to if you wanted to do these things?
- a  see wildlife  _East Africa, Namibia_
- b  see beautiful scenery  _____
- c  do exciting activities  _____
- d  go on a relaxing boat trip  _____
- e  climb a mountain  _____

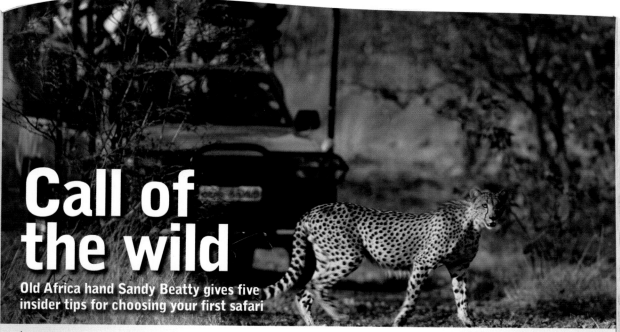

# Call of the wild

**Old Africa hand Sandy Beatty gives five insider tips for choosing your first safari**

[1] The dry season offers better game-viewing, as higher concentrations of animals congregate around fewer waterholes, with less foliage to hide behind. During the rains, some tracks become impassable and many camps close. However, in the wet season, animals – and consequently safari vehicles – are often more dispersed. Trees and shrubs are greener and in flower, and many newborn animals can be spotted. Weather's not the only consideration – visiting Kenya or Tanzania during the Great Migration (July–September), when more than one million wildebeest thunder across the Serengeti, is an experience of a lifetime.

[2] There's nothing quite like a top-end safari lodge for the classic Africa experience – crisp white tablecloths, cold drinks, impeccable service and usually a waterhole, or savannah viewpoint not too far away. But camping safaris get you right in among the action. Either way, with Explore* you will have a top-notch leader and you'll be spotting the same game – there's no such thing as a luxury lion.

[3] A 4WD game drive enables you to sample several different areas in a relatively short space of time. But walking safaris get you away from trails to enjoy the smaller creatures and quieter sounds of the bush. Boat safaris get you close to animals drinking from waterholes and rivers, and offer a unique perspective. For the ideal mix, why not combine more than one mode of transport?

[4] If you have a burning ambition to spot one particular species, check where to head for the best chance. For apes and the Great Migration, it has to be East Africa; for desert-adapted elephants or a close-up cheetah encounter, Namibia's the place. Trip dossiers will give you an idea of which species you can expect to see.

[5] Africa offers a lot more than just safaris. Head for Tanzania to tack on a Zanzibar beach break or to climb Kilimanjaro; to Zambia for Victoria Falls and some adrenalin action; to Kenya for Arab culture and dhow cruises; or to South Africa for fantastic landscapes, food and wine.

*Explore is a travel company.

**7 Look at the headings in Exercise 3. Imagine you are going on safari. What are your own answers to the five questions in the headings?**

### Class bonus

Work with a partner. Ask and answer questions about your safari. For example, *When are you going to go? Are you going to camp?* Find out if you have chosen the same type of safari holiday as your partner. Work with several other students and find the person whose holiday plans are most similar to your own.

### Focus on ...
**vocabulary**

abc**d**ef

There are some useful words about safari holidays in the article. Read these definitions of some of the words and write each word.

a  wild animals (that are hunted or photographed) g a m e
b  a small house in the country that is used especially by people on a sporting holiday _ _ _ _ _
c  a path through the countryside _ _ _ _ _
d  wild parts of Africa where very few people live

   _ _ _  _ _ _ _
e  a group of animals which share the same characteristics

   _ _ _ _ _ _ _ _
f  an animal like a large monkey _ _ _ _

## B  A walk in the park

**1** You are going to read part of a magazine article which has the title 'A walk in the park'. Choose the correct adjective from the box to complete the sentence and find the meaning of the expression.

| | | |
|---|---|---|
| boring | cheap | difficult |
| easy | frightening | tiring |

'A walk in the park' is something that is ............................... to do.

**2** Look quickly at the introduction to the article. Which park is the walk in?

............................................................

### Learning tip

Journalists often begin factual magazine articles with dramatic true stories to catch the reader's attention. They give the factual information later. To tell these true stories, journalists might use direct speech, past tenses and personal pronouns (*I, he, we,* etc.). Look out for these things in an article and then you will be able to recognize which parts of it are the dramatic beginning and which parts give the factual information.

**3** Read the first seven paragraphs of the article. How does the journalist, Narina, begin her article? Tick ✓ one of the boxes.

a  She describes the Olifants Trail. ☐

b  She describes why she chose the trail. ☐

c  She describes what happened one day. ☐

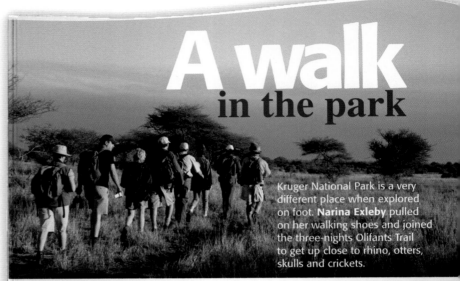

# A walk
## in the park

Kruger National Park is a very different place when explored on foot. **Narina Exleby** pulled on her walking shoes and joined the three-nights Olifants Trail to get up close to rhino, otters, skulls and crickets.

**1** "That's your bush. If it charges, you get behind it," Nicol Coetsee whispered softly. Eight pairs of eyes widened behind him. The white rhino munched on sweet grass. Everyone stood still.

**2** It's one thing for a rhino to pass three metres from your vehicle, but when you're watching it graze just 15 metres away from you, and you have only a flimsy piece of vegetation for cover, the feeling is quite different. When it turns and charges, and you have a 2,600 kilogram white rhino bull sprinting straight at you, it's blood chilling.

**3** The ground shook and thundered and dust billowed up behind the rhino. As the distance between it and the vegetation grew shorter and shorter, everyone held their breath and stood dead still; you could have heard a butterfly land on a twig.

**4** When Nicol and Tsambok – both trail rangers – shouted and waved their arms, the rhino realised we were humans, took fright and sprinted off in another direction. Once the dust had settled, Nicol explained it had been a case of mistaken identity – we weren't really the rhino's target. Someone in the group had coughed and, probably thinking it was another male in its territory, the rhino had hurtled over to enforce its territorial rights.

**5** It's the kind of encounter people dream of – and dread – when they do a wilderness trail.

**6** Wilderness trails in Kruger National Park offer three nights of bush solitude. There are seven wilderness areas, set aside for walking trails. These sections have been virtually untouched by humans. Each has a camp, which is basic but comfortable, and minimal roads – used only by a few trail staff.

**7** Olifants Trail Camp is situated on the banks of the Olifants River. In the pre-dawn mornings you'll wake up to the snorts of hippos. During the day, the call of a fish eagle pierces the midday heat and at night the moans and roars of lions drift into the camp.

**4** In which paragraph does Narina finish the dramatic beginning of her article?

-------------------------------------------------

**5** What are the remaining paragraphs about?

-------------------------------------------------

**6** Look at the map and find the rhino. When did Narina see it? Tick ✓ one of the boxes.

a  On the first morning. ☐
b  On the first afternoon. ☐
c  On the second morning. ☐
d  On the second afternoon. ☐

**7** What happened when the group saw the rhino? Put these events in the correct order.

a  Someone in the group coughed and the rhino heard this. ☐
b  They saw a rhino 15 metres away. ☐1
c  The rhino ran off in another direction. ☐
d  Nicol told them what to do if the rhino charged. ☐
e  Nicol and Tsambok shouted and waved their arms. ☐
f  The rhino turned and ran towards the group. ☐

**8** Why might people 'dream of – and dread' the situation Narina has just described? How would you have felt?

**9** What would the rangers have done if the rhino had not run away? Have they ever had to do this? Read two later paragraphs from the article and find out.

-------------------------------------------------

> Whenever we walked, the two trail rangers carried .458 calibre rifles. The group moved in single file with Nicol and Tsambok in front. "If we got into a dangerous situation, this would be the best position to be in," Nicol explained. "If Tsambok or I were at the back of the group, we would have to fire past eight people. Because we walk into the wind, the animals behind us or to our left or right are aware of our presence. It's the ones in front of us we have to worry about – the ones that we might stumble across and frighten."

**Campfire talk**

Around the dying campfire late one night, someone asked Nicol if he'd ever had any "funny incidents" with a group – a probing question that led to "so, have you ever had to use your gun?" One he must get asked often.

Nicol's eyes darkened. "Twice – incidents with elephants." His words were sketchy and his hands fidgeted. This was no fireside tale of bravado; this was the way life had to be in the bush. "I wouldn't have shot if I had been on my own." And he quietly left it at that.

**10** Would you like to go on the Olifants Trail? Why? / Why not?

E ✗tra practice

Which animal in this unit would you most like to see? Find out about it on the Internet. Try the website www.animal.discovery.com

**Can-do checklist**

Tick what you can do.

|  | Can do | Need more practice |
|---|---|---|
| I can identify the main point in a paragraph. | ✓ | ✓ |
| I can identify a dramatic beginning to an article. | | |
| I can follow the order of events in a narrative. | | |

# Unit 8

# In the newspapers

go to Useful language p. 84

---

**Get ready to** **read**

- How often do you read a newspaper? .................................................................................

- Which of these sections of the newspaper do you read? Which do you read first? Why?
  TECHNOLOGY      CULTURE AND REVIEW    SPORT    NEWS
  FINANCIAL AND BUSINESS    HEALTH AND MEDICAL    TRAVEL

- Which sports are covered in the Sport section of the newspaper you read?
  .................................................................................

---

## A Bikes are everywhere!

**1 You are going to read the first part of three articles about cycling. Before you read, think about the newspaper sections in *Get ready to read*. What could a cycling article in each of the sections be about?**

> An article in the Technology section could be about the latest developments in bike design.

**2 Skim each extract on the opposite page and match it with one of the newspaper sections in *Get ready to read*.**

Extract 1 ..........................
Extract 2 ..........................
Extract 3 ..........................

**3 Read each extract and circle the words so that the sentences are true.**

a 'Cooke shows ingredients for big prize' because *she is very fit / she has had a very successful season*.

b 'Cyclists facing £2,500 bell fines' could apply to *anyone who cycles / people who frequently cycle* without a bell.

c Andrew Ritchie has spent *a long time / a short time* developing 'The bicycle that turned into folding money'.

### Did you know ...?

British and American daily newspapers, such as *The Independent* and *The Washington Post*, usually have a related Sunday equivalent – *The Independent on Sunday* and *The Washington Post Sunday Edition*. Sunday newspapers contain more sections and pages than daily newspapers. The 14 September 1987 edition of *The Sunday New York Times* weighed more than 5.4 kg and contained 1,612 pages.

### Learning tip

Newspapers contain an enormous number and variety of reading texts, but most people do not read a newspaper from cover to cover. What we read depends on what we are interested in. We look at headlines, which summarize articles, and either read the article – part of it or all of it, again depending on our interest – or move on to another article. We read selectively.

**4 Which is the most difficult extract for you to read? Think about the following:**

- unknown words
- long words
- long sentences
- unfamiliar grammatical structures
- background information needed
- complicated order of information

**5 Choose one of the extracts and read it carefully. List the main points.**

.................................................................................
.................................................................................
.................................................................................

1

CYCLING WORLD CHAMPIONSHIPS

# Cooke shows ingredients for big prize

**by Jeremy Whittle**

Is there any race that Nicole Cooke, the wonderfully talented cyclist from Wales cannot win? The 23-year-old will discover the answer to that question in Austria this week when she aims for an elusive World Championship crown.

Cooke will lead Team GB in Salzburg this week, at the climax of a phenomenal season during which she has emphasised her standing as the leading cyclist of her generation.

This year Cooke has risen to the top of the world rankings (the first British cyclist to do so), won the women's Tour de France, the World Cup series, the British National Championship, the Tour of New Zealand and several other significant events.

Apart from when she has had knee injuries, it has always been this way for Cooke. In 2001, she won world titles in road racing, time trialling and mountain biking. However, that triple crown came as a junior and a women's world title continues to elude her.

Full cycle: Cooke is favourite for success in Salzburg this week

2

# Cyclists facing £2,500 bell fines

**Tim Shipman**

Cyclists could face fines of up to £2,500 for riding without a bell. New laws being considered by the Government would mean that every bike in Britain would have to be fitted with a bell.

Cycling without one would be a criminal offence, the same as dangerous riding, ignoring red lights or cycling on the pavement.

These offences typically attract fines of between £30 and £60.

But persistent offenders can be fined up to £2,500, have their driving licence endorsed or, in extreme cases, be jailed for 2 years.

Under current regulations, every bicycle has to be sold with a bell fitted. But there is no obligation for the rider to keep the bell after purchase.

Transport Minister Stephen Ladyman has now said it would be 'sensible' to extend cycling penalties to ensure that bells are not removed.

Sound advice: New bikes are fitted with bells, but there is nothing in law to stop cyclists removing them

3

# The bicycle that turned into folding money

**Ben Laurance meets Andrew Ritchie, an obsessive who has steered a portable bike into a British manufacturing success story**

Meet Andrew Ritchie for the first time, and take in what you see: a lean, middle-aged man, slightly dishevelled, with one leg of his brown corduroy trousers tucked into his sock.

You might guess that he is a slightly posh gardener who has just cycled back from his latest landscaping project: he has something of the outdoor air about him. The tucked-in trouser leg gives him away as a cyclist.

And you would not be completely wrong. Yes, Andrew Ritchie used to be a landscape gardener. And yes, he's certainly a cyclist: each day, he pedals the six-and-a-bit miles from his home in South Kensington, west London to work on an unprepossessing industrial estate near Junction 2 of the M4.

But Ritchie, 58, is more than just another cyclist. He is a self-confessed obsessive, someone who has devoted the past 30 years of his life to building the best portable bicycle in the world, a machine that is fun and efficient to ride but can be quickly folded into a package smaller than an average suitcase, carried up and down stairs, tucked behind a train seat or secreted under a desk.

And it is an obsession that has reaped rewards. Ritchie controls and runs Brompton Bicycle, one of only two volume manufacturers still making bikes in Britain. No, it will never be on the scale of Raleigh, which in its heyday was producing a million frames a year and whose bikes are now imported. But since its inception, Brompton has made almost 100,000 of its distinctive 'folders'. It aims to produce nearly 14,000 in the coming year. It is a rarity – a British manufacturing success story.

6 Would you be interested in reading the rest of any of these articles? Why? / Why not? Would you rather choose an article of your own? What would that article be about?

**Class bonus**

Read the other extracts. Lightly underline any words or phrases that you don't understand. Work with a partner. Ask your friend if he/she knows the meaning of the text you have underlined. Help each other to understand the articles.

# B Should I wear a helmet?

**1 Label the picture with the words in the box.**

> cycle panniers    cycle path    fluorescent jacket    ~~helmet~~    lights

**2 How can we make cycling safer? Tick ✓ one or more of the boxes.**

Every cyclist should …
a … have a bell on their bike. ☐
b … cycle on the pavement. ☐
c … wear a helmet. ☐
d … ride on a cycle path. ☐
e … ignore traffic lights. ☐
f … have lights on their bike. ☐
g … wear fluorescent clothing. ☐
h … carry things in proper cycle panniers. ☐

a .......... helmet ..........
e ..........................
b ..........................
d ..........................
c ..........................

**3 Look at the headline of the newspaper article below. Does this headline surprise you? Why? / Why not?**

# Cyclists with helmets 'more likely to be hit'

By **Ray Massey**
Transport Editor

Cyclists who wear helmets are more likely to be hit by overtaking vehicles, psychologists said last night.

Research reveals motorists drive more than three inches* closer to cyclists in helmets because they see them as more experienced.

However, female cyclists are given more room on the road than male cyclists, according to the survey.

The findings are being published by traffic psychologist Dr Ian Walker from the University of Bath. He used a bicycle fitted with an ultrasonic distance sensor to record data from more than 2,500 overtaking motorists.

After carrying out tests in Salisbury and Bristol, he said drivers were twice as likely to get closer to his bike when he had a helmet on.

Dr Walker said: 'This was something I had suspected, as many cyclists had told me of similar experiences.

'The perception is that those wearing helmets are more experienced and more predictable.

'Drivers think, "He knows what he's doing, he won't do anything surprising". But that's really quite a dangerous thought, particularly as so many cycling novices are told to wear helmets.'

Dr Walker was struck twice during the experiment.

**Rider risk: Vehicles drive closer**

Buses and trucks were the worst offenders. While the average car gave cyclists 52 inches of room, trucks got 7.5 inches closer and buses 9 inches.

Dr Walker wore a long wig to see if there was any difference in passing distance when vehicles thought they were overtaking a female cyclist. Vehicles gave him an average 6 inches more space.

He said this may be because women are seen as less predictable road users or because female cyclists are more rare and therefore treated with more caution.

Dr Walker wants his research to raise awareness of the dangers facing cyclists on busy roads.

Although road fatalities generally have fallen to a record low, cyclist deaths rose by an alarming ten per cent last year, official casualty figures revealed in June.

The number of riders killed in Britain increased to 148 in 2005 – the highest level since 1999.

The number seriously injured rose by two per cent to 2,212. Total casualties among cyclists, including those slightly injured, fell by one per cent in 2005 to 16,561.

Experts blame the rise in cycling deaths on the boom in the inexperienced 'green' riders taking to the road to beat congestion, reduce pollution and get fit.

Overtaking cars are thought to be the most dangerous hazard for riders. Dr Walker said: 'We know from research that many drivers see cyclists as a separate subculture to which they don't belong.

'I hope drivers realise they are making assumptions about cyclists based on their appearance.

'If as a result of this study there were less injuries on the roads, that would be wonderful.'

Despite his findings, cyclists who wear helmets are more likely to survive a collision with a car, so the increased risk of an accident could be outweighed by the chances of living through it.

*1 inch = 2.5 centimetres

**4** Journalists often start a newspaper article with the main topic to attract the reader's attention. In the article on the opposite page the main topic is given in the first sentence. What do the next two sentences do? Match the sentences with the functions.

Sentence 2      gives contrasting information.
Sentence 3      gives more details about the main topic.
                gives a reason for the behaviour described in the main topic.

**5** Read the article carefully and find out more details about the research. Complete the chart.

| Who carried out the research? | Dr Ian Walker, a traffic psychologist |
|---|---|
| Where? | |
| How? | |
| Why? | |

**6** Complete the sentences which summarize the main points of the article.

a  Overtaking drivers get closer to cyclists who _wear helmets._
b  They think these cyclists are ...............................................................................
c  Drivers give more space to ...............................................................................
d  ............................................................... get closer to cyclists than other vehicles.
e  In 2005 the number of cyclists who died in road accidents in Britain
     ...............................................................................
f  More people have started cycling to ...............................................................................
g  Cyclists who wear helmets have a better chance of ...............................................................................

**7** Do any of the main points surprise you?

**8** Do you think cyclists should stop wearing helmets? Why? / Why not?

**Focus on ...**
**synonyms**

Complete this sentence from the article. The two missing words are synonyms – they have the same or a similar meaning.
Although road ........................ generally have fallen to a record low, cyclist ........................ rose by an alarming ten per cent last year, official casualty figures revealed in June.

The following words are all in the article. Circle the words in each list which are synonyms.
a  (cyclists)  motorists  (riders)
b  hit  struck  injured
c  overtaking  carrying out  passing
d  room  space  boom
e  data  perception  thought
f  suspected  rose  increased
g  test  experiment  risk
h  caution  collision  accident

Find the remaining words in the article and try and work out a synonym for each one. (Synonyms for some of them are in the article.)
a  _motorists – drivers_
b  ...............................................................................
c  ...............................................................................
d  ...............................................................................
e  ...............................................................................
f  ...............................................................................
g  ...............................................................................
h  ...............................................................................

**Can-do checklist**

Tick what you can do.

|  | Can do | Need more practice |
|---|---|---|
| I can identify newspaper sections and articles from these sections. | ✓ | ✓ |
| I can read a newspaper selectively. | | |
| I can find the main points in a newspaper article. | | |

# Review 1
## Units 1–8

**A Are these statements true (T) or false (F)?**

1 You should read every word of a text in order to find the information that you are looking for. ...... (Unit 1)

2 We sometimes scan a text to find a particular word, and then read the text around the word. ...... (Unit 2)

3 You should always approach a text as if you were reading it in the real world. ...... (Unit 3)

4 When we skim a text, we read every word. ...... (Unit 4)

5 We can use a variety of reading skills to read the same piece of text. ...... (Unit 5)

6 Texts are easier to understand if you know nothing about the topic before you begin to read. ...... (Unit 6)

7 Magazine articles usually begin by setting the scene and providing all the background information. ...... (Unit 7)

8 A newspaper headline usually summarizes the main point of the article. ...... (Unit 8)

**B Now read the *Learning tips* for Units 1–8 on pages 87–9. Do you want to change any of your answers in Exercise A?**

**C Skim Texts A–D on the opposite page. Decide which text each of these people would read. Write the letter of the text(s) in the box.**

9 someone who has been out all day and has just got home [ ]

10 someone who is planning a holiday abroad [ ]

11 someone who wants to make a hot drink [ ]

12 someone who is returning home after studying in Britain [ ]

**D Read Texts A1 and A2 and tick ✓ the correct boxes in the chart.**

| | | Cocoa powder | Drinking chocolate |
|---|---|---|---|
| 13 | This product already contains sugar. | | |
| 14 | This product weighs less than the other. | | |
| 15 | You need more of this product to make a drink. | | |
| 16 | You need to use some cold milk to make this drink. | | |
| 17 | This product costs less. | | |

**E Read Text B. Complete these sentences.**

18 ..................... people use mountain bikes in New Zealand than touring bikes.

19 You ..................... always borrow a bike from the hostel you're staying in.

20 If you want a bike for three or four weeks, it's ..................... expensive to rent than to buy.

21 Cyclists in New Zealand ..................... wear a helmet.

22 A cycle shop may give you back ..................... the amount you paid for a bike at the end of your trip.

**F Carlos has contacted Excess Baggage PLC about transporting his baggage to Spain. Read Text C and decide if these sentences are true (T) or false (F).**

23 This company transports baggage only to countries in Europe. ......

24 Carlos's baggage may travel by lorry to Spain. ......

25 If his baggage is very heavy, it is probably better to send it by road or ship. ......

26 He won't have to pay extra to use the company's packaging. ......

27 If Carlos can't lift one of his packages, it probably weighs more than the maximum allowed. ......

**G Read Text D and put events a–e in order.**

28 [ ]  29 [ ]  30 [ ]  31 [ ]  32 [ ]

a Tom read the electricity meter and completed the back of the card.

b Tom came home and saw the card that had been left.

c Tom went off to college the following morning.

d Tom put the card in the window near the front door.

e On 29 June someone came to check how much electricity Tom had used.

# Help prevent fire

Fire is always a threat, but you can help prevent it.

## Use lighting and heaters safely

Make sure nothing that could burn is too close to lamps or heaters. Make sure that radiant parts on heaters are not exposed.

## Respect electricity

It can cause shocks and fires. Do not use a damaged lead or plug. If required, turn off electrical appliances when leaving them unattended.

## Clean up clutter

Rubbish may help start a fire or make a small fire bigger.

## Take care with smoking materials

Smoking is not allowed on these premises. If you do smoke, smoke outside the building and only where it is allowed. Dispose of all matches and cigarette butts carefully in metal containers.

## Store combustible materials safely

Don't keep them on escape routes, staircases or underneath enclosed staircases.

## Don't block fire exits, escape routes or alarm call points

Make sure fire exits are free from obstructions and are not locked, chained or bolted. Don't leave large items in corridors, or near staircases, or in front of alarm call points.

## Keep all fire doors shut

Never wedge them open.

---

### Know the fire drill

Learn in advance:

- the location and operation of the nearest fire exit and alternative exits
- what you should do when you hear the fire alarm
- your assembly point in case you need to leave the building

---

**5** Four of the compound nouns with *fire* from *Get ready to read* are in the text. Scan the text and find them. What is each one? Use a dictionary if you need to.

1 A fire exit is a special door that people use to leave the building if there is a fire.

2 ........................................................

........................................................

3 ........................................................

........................................................

4 ........................................................

........................................................

........................................................

### Learning tip

Dictionaries – both bilingual and monolingual – are very useful when you are learning a language. However, try not to use them too much. When you are reading, try to work out the meaning of an unknown word. Think about the other words around it, the word class it belongs to (e.g. noun, verb), similar words you know in English and similar words in your own language. Then use the dictionary to check that you have worked out the meaning of the word correctly.

**6** Find these words in the leaflet and try to work out their meaning. Then check your answers in a dictionary. Remember to check the pronunciation of the words too.

radiant plug electrical appliances premises dispose combustible obstructions wedge

### Class bonus

In pairs, discuss fire safety at workplaces you know. Are these places safe? What could be done to make them safer? Write a list of points in English.

## B Fire safety procedures

1 Skim the notice on the right. Add one of these words to the title.

> alarm  brigade  door  drill  exit

2 Read the sub-headings. Can you work out the meanings of *suspect* and *intermittent*?

3 The text mentions an 'alarm call point' and an 'assembly point'? What are these? What does *point* mean in these expressions?

-----------------------------------------
-----------------------------------------
-----------------------------------------

4 Read the whole text and <u>underline</u> any words you don't understand. Then read the text again carefully and try to work out the meaning of these words. Remember to use the strategies in the *Learning tip* on page 47.

### Did you know ...?

If you need to phone for the Fire Brigade in the UK, you can call 999 or 112. These are also the numbers for the other Emergency Services – police and ambulance. 112 is used throughout the European Union. Emergency numbers in other English-speaking countries are:

| | |
|---|---|
| USA | 911 |
| Canada | 911 |
| Australia | 000 |
| New Zealand | 111 |
| South Africa | 112 |

# Fire

**If you discover a fire or see smoke and suspect there is a fire**

1 Shout 'FIRE!' to warn people in the immediate vicinity.

2 Sound the alarm by breaking the glass at the nearest alarm call point.

3 Go to Reception and report to the Person in Control, or to the Fire Brigade and Rescue Services when they arrive.

**If you are in the building and hear the intermittent fire alarm**

1 Continue working but be prepared to leave the building should the continuous alarm sound. Close all windows.

2 Do not use the lifts when you are moving around the building.

**If you are in the building and hear the continuous fire alarm**

1 Leave the building by the nearest exit not affected by the fire. If you are responsible for any visitors, ensure they leave with you and attend assembly point G. Those with mobile telephones should take them with them. Do not stop to collect personal belongings, coats, bags, etc.

2 Those in charge of departments or their deputies should briefly search their areas to ensure that the immediate vicinity is clear of staff and visitors.

3 When vacating the building, do not use the lifts.

4 Go to your assembly point.

5 Departmental heads or their deputies should ensure that all members of staff are accounted for.

6 If you believe anyone to be unaccounted for, report this to the Person in Control.

**Assembly points**
G Ground floor staff and visitors
1 First floor staff
2 Second floor staff
3 Third floor staff

**5 Read the first two sets of instructions and choose the correct answers.**

a If you see a fire, you should
1 shout 'Fire!' to the people who are near you. ☐
2 run around the building shouting 'Fire!' ☐
3 shout 'Fire!' to people outside in the street. ☐

b When you break the glass of the alarm call point, you
1 make the fire alarm stop. ☐
2 make the fire alarm ring. ☐
3 make the fire alarm sound louder. ☐

c If the intermittent alarm sounds, you should
1 use the stairs instead of the lift. ☐
2 leave the building. ☐
3 turn off your computer. ☐

d You should close all windows
1 so that nobody can get into the building. ☐
2 so that the noise won't disturb people outside. ☐
3 so that air can't get in and spread the fire. ☐

---

**Focus on ...**
**compound nouns**

A compound noun consists of two nouns, for example, *fire alarm*. Here are six compound nouns which begin with *fire*. These compound nouns are written as one word. Match the words with the definitions.

| firearm   firefighter   fireplace   firewall   firewood   ~~firework~~ |
| --- |

a a small object that explodes to produce a loud noise and bright colours ....firework....
b someone whose job is to put out fires ....................
c a gun that you can carry easily ....................
d wood that is used for burning on a fire ....................
e a space in the wall of a room where you can have a fire, or the structure around this space ....................
f a system that stops other people looking at information on your computer while it is connected to the Internet ....................

---

**6 Read the third set of instructions. What should you do if you hear the continuous fire alarm in these situations?**

a Your desk is on the ground floor, and you are having a meeting at your desk with two people from another company.
*You should ensure your visitors leave with you and you should go to assembly point G.*

b You work on the first floor.
.................................................................
.................................................................

c Your mobile phone is in the top drawer of your desk.
.................................................................

d You are playing tennis after work, and your sports bag is under your desk.
.................................................................

e You are head of your department. Everyone in your department has left their desks and you are getting ready to leave.
.................................................................

f You are acting as head of your department. You are at your assembly point.
.................................................................

g When you get to the assembly point, you can't see one of your colleagues.
.................................................................
.................................................................

---

**E✗tra practice**

This unit has been about fire in the workplace. Go to www.firekills.gov.uk and click on Fire safety advice. Read the webpage Check your home and follow the advice. How safe is your home?

---

**Can-do checklist**

Tick what you can do.

| | Can do | Need more practice |
| --- | --- | --- |
| I can work out the meaning of unknown words from the context. | ✔ | ✔ |
| I can understand a leaflet about preventing a fire. | | |
| I can follow instructions for a fire drill. | | |

# Unit 10
## Lines of communication

**Get ready to** read

- Circle the words in these sentences so that they are true for you.
  I would rather *speak* / *write* to someone than *speak* / *write* to them.
  My preferred method of communicating in writing is *by email* / *by letter*.
  I get *over* / *fewer than* 50 emails every day.
  I always try to respond to an email *the same day* / *within a few days*.
  I *am on some* / *am not on any* email mailing lists.

- How do you organize your emails? Write *Y* (yes) or *N* (no).
  Do you put them in different folders? ......
  Do you delete them regularly? ......
  Do you keep printed copies of your emails? ......
  Do you copy them into your To Do list or calendar? ......

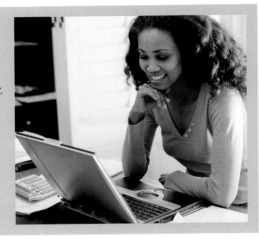

go to Useful language p. 85

## A I copied you in

**Learning tip**

When you read an email, find out who it is from and who it is for. Sometimes the message is just for you, sometimes it is for you as a member of a group, and sometimes you are copied in (cc = carbon copy, i.e. you are sent a copy of an email which has been sent primarily to someone else). If you know who the email has been sent to, you will know whether you have to reply, or take some kind of action.

**1** Isabel Senna and Emma Wright both work for Bishops in Wellington, New Zealand. Isabel has received emails a–c. Who are they from and who are they to? Circle the names.

**2** Why has Isabel been sent emails a–c? Match the emails with their purpose.

| | |
|---|---|
| Email a | requests something. |
| Email b | makes a suggestion. |
| Email c | gives some information. |

**3** What exactly is the request, the suggestion and the information in emails a–c?

**a**
From: Emma Wright
To: Isabel Senna, Dan Vettori
cc:
Date/time: 11/10   9.25
Subject: Meeting with Jane cancelled

Isabel and Dan
Jane has just called to say that she is off sick today and won't be able to meet you both this afternoon. She sends her apologies. She probably won't be back in now until next week. Thanks,
Emma

**b**
From: Rotha Lim
To: Emma Wright, Isabel Senna
cc: Ben Parker
Date/time: 11/10   11.15
Subject: Conference folders

Hi there
Would you be available one day next week? Marketing have asked for help with making conference folders and getting things ready to be shipped to Wanaka before the beginning of November. If you work together, it should only take one afternoon. Let me know which and I'll try to join you.
Rotha

**c**
From: Dan Vettori
To: Isabel Senna
cc:
Date/time: 11/10   14.05
Subject: Meeting with Jane

Isabel
If Jane's back, is next Tuesday any good for you? Morning or afternoon, I don't mind. I'm off to Auckland on Wednesday with Greg for three days, so would prefer to meet before then.
Dan

## Class bonus

Write Isabel's reply email to either Rotha or Dan. Then find someone who has written the other reply and exchange emails. Respond to the email you have received from this person.

**4** Read emails d–f quickly. Who are they from and who are they to? (Circle) the names.

**5** Why do you think Isabel has been copied in on emails d–f? Write sentences.

Email d  She has been copied in so that she knows Paul, Rotha, Greg, Jane and Dan are aware that she will do anything urgent the following week.

Email e  _____

_____

Email f  _____

_____

## Focus on ...
### collocations

A collocation is the combination of two or more words which often go together, for example, *send (my / his,* etc.) *apologies, working lunch.*

Find three verbs which go with the noun *meeting* in emails a–f. Use them to complete these sentences.

a  You _____ a meeting if you say that it will not happen.

b  You _____ a meeting if you arrange it for a certain time.

c  You can _____ a meeting if you say that it will happen at a later time.

Find two other collocations with *meeting* and complete these sentences.

d  Isabel will bring the food to the _____

_____ .

e  The _____ _____ will take place on 16 October.

**6** Email f doesn't say why the team meeting has been postponed. Which of the other emails suggests a possible reason? What is it?

_____

**7** What do you learn about the team Isabel works with? Who is doing what next week?

## Did you know ...?

Wellington is the capital of New Zealand. It is at the southern end of North Island. Wanaka is a lakeside resort town in the south of South Island.

d

From: Emma Wright
To: Paul Collingwood, Rotha Lim, Greg Kawana, Jane Reed, Dan Vettori
cc: Isabel Senna
Date/time: 11/10   14.40
Subject: Holiday next week

Dear Team
I am out of the office next week, but will be back on 22 October. If you had anything you wanted me to do next week that can be done now, please let me know.
Isabel has kindly agreed to cover anything urgent while I'm away.
Emma

e

From: Emma Wright
To: Paul Collingwood
cc: Isabel Senna
Date/time: 11/10   15.15
Subject: Lunch for Monday

Paul
I have managed to book lunch for Monday 15th.
They are providing a working lunch of sandwiches, crisps and fruit for six people along with water and orange juice. The food has to be collected at 11.45 from the canteen. I have asked Isabel to do that for you. She will bring it to your meeting room.
Thanks
Emma

f

From: Emma Wright
To: Jane Reed, Rotha Lim, Greg Kawana
cc: Paul Collingwood, Isabel Senna
Date/time: 11/10   15.50
Subject: Team meeting postponed

Dear all
The team meeting scheduled for next Monday morning has been postponed. It will now take place next Tuesday (16 October), at 11.00 am, in Meeting Room 2. I won't be there, but Isabel will attend.
Thanks
Emma

# B Leaving and joining

**1 Read the email and then match a–c with the correct names.**

|  | Emma |
|---|---|
| a It's from | Greg |
|  | Dan |
| b It's to | Isabel |
|  | Jane |
| c It's about | Paul |
|  | Rotha |

**2 How does Paul feel about the news? Tick ✓ one of the boxes.**

a He is happy that Emma is leaving. ☐
b He is sorry that she is leaving. ☐
c He is pleased for Emma, but sorry. ☐

**3 Circle the correct words in these sentences.**

a Emma's new job is with another *company / department*.
b She is leaving *at the end of the next week / in a week's time*.
c She has worked for the company *for three years / since Paul joined*.

**4 Read the notice that Paul puts on the office noticeboard. Match the paragraphs with topics a–e.**

a her personal qualities ☐
b the positions Emma has had ☐
c the announcement ☐1☐
d good wishes for the future ☐
e the work she has done ☐

**5 Read the notice again and answer the questions.**

a What is Emma's current job title?
------------------------------------
b What does she do in her current job?
------------------------------------
c What other positions has she had at Bishops? ------------------
d What is her new job going to be?
------------------------------------

## E✗tra practice

Are there any notices in English on the noticeboard where you work or study? If not, where can you find notices in English in your town / city? What are they about?

---

From: Paul Collingwood
To: Jane Reed, Rotha Lim, Greg Kawana, Dan Vettori, Isabel Senna
cc:
Date/time: 6/11   10.45
Subject: Emma Wright

Dear Colleagues
It is with mixed emotions that I pass on this news – Emma has resigned! She is leaving us to take up a job with Lynams in Napier. Her last day in the office will be the 17th (next Friday). I know Emma will be missed by all of us at Bishops who have worked closely with her over the last three years, but at the same time I can understand that this is a wonderful opportunity. I am sure that Emma will thoroughly enjoy the challenge her new job offers.
All best wishes
Paul

---

Date: 8 November

1 Emma Wright is leaving Bishops to take up the role of Recruitment Administrator at Lynams in Napier. Her last day in the office is Friday 16 November.

2 Emma has been working with us for more than three years. She started as a temporary keyboard operator on a six-month contract and then took on a permanent position as an administration assistant. Eighteen months ago she was promoted to the position of Office Administrator.

3 Emma has fantastic computer skills and under her direction we now know our PCs much better than we used to! Emma excelled herself in setting up a superb website, which has proved immensely successful. She has also updated the database on a regular basis, and taken over responsibilities for publicity and producing promotional items such as pens and notepads.

4 Emma is an invaluable member of the team and we will miss her enthusiasm and good humour greatly. Over the years Emma has been a tremendous friend and colleague to many of us here in Wellington and a welcome point of contact for our customers and suppliers.

5 I am sure you will want to join me in wishing her every success in her new career.

Paul Collingwood
Project & Development Manager

**6** Look at this list of typical events that can take place when someone leaves a job. What usually happens in your country? Tick ✓ one or more of the boxes.

a  The person who is leaving provides cakes. ☐
b  Colleagues provide cakes. ☐
c  Everyone signs a card for the person who is leaving. ☐
d  The staff give money and buy a present for the person who is leaving. ☐
e  There is a small leaving party in the office and the boss makes a speech. ☐
f  People all go out for a drink or a meal with the person who is leaving. ☐

**7** Read the email from Emma and <u>underline</u> the events in Exercise 6 which are true for her.

---

**Emma Wright**

| **To:** | Paul Collingwood, Jane Reed, Rotha Lim, Greg Kawana, Dan Vettori |
| | 10/11   14.00 |
| **cc:** | Isabel Senna |
| **Subject:** | Leaving do |

Dear Friends and Colleagues

As you know, I'm leaving next week and moving away from Wellington. There will be coffee and cakes (which my mum has baked) at 4.30 pm next Friday in the coffee area. Also, Isabel has booked a table at my favourite Chinese restaurant (Uncle Chang's, 72 Courtenay Place), for 7.30 that evening. Please let her know if you can come along. Everyone is welcome!

I know some of you will be at the Sales Conference in Wanaka next week. If I don't see you before I go, take care and thanks for being such good colleagues these last three years!

Best wishes
Emma

---

**8** Read another notice that Paul has put on the noticeboard. Is someone else leaving Bishops? Who is Vincent Ingram?

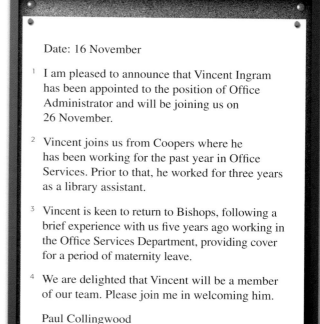

Date: 16 November

1  I am pleased to announce that Vincent Ingram has been appointed to the position of Office Administrator and will be joining us on 26 November.

2  Vincent joins us from Coopers where he has been working for the past year in Office Services. Prior to that, he worked for three years as a library assistant.

3  Vincent is keen to return to Bishops, following a brief experience with us five years ago working in the Office Services Department, providing cover for a period of maternity leave.

4  We are delighted that Vincent will be a member of our team. Please join me in welcoming him.

Paul Collingwood
Project & Development Manager

**9** Match functions a–d with the paragraphs in the notice about Vincent.

a  giving information about work history     paragraph 1
b  encouraging staff to welcome someone    paragraph 2
c  announcing a change in personnel         paragraph 3
d  describing previous in-house experience  paragraph 4

**10** Do you think Vincent will enjoy working at Bishops? Why? / Why not?

**Can-do checklist**

Tick what you can do.

|  | Can do | Need more practice |
| --- | --- | --- |
| I can work out who an email is from and who it is to. | ✓ | ✓ |
| I can work out the main purpose of an email. | | |
| I can understand resignation and appointment notices. | | |

# Unit 11
## Any comments?

go to Useful language p. 85

---

**Get ready to** **read**

- Have you ever been asked to fill in a questionnaire? What was it about?
  Tick ✓ one or more of the boxes.
  something you had bought ☐          conditions at work ☐
  facilities or services in a town ☐    other (specify what) ..................
  a holiday ☐

- If you wrote about the feedback from some questionnaires, which
  of these would you include? Tick ✓ one or more of the boxes.
  a  a description of how you devised the questionnaire ☐
  b  information about how long it took to devise ☐
  c  an analysis of the feedback ☐
  d  conclusions from the feedback ☐
  e  recommendations for changes based on the feedback ☐
  f  recommendations for future questionnaires ☐

## A Holiday questionnaire

1  Ivana works for Mountain Travel, a British
   travel company that arranges holidays in
   Europe. As part of her job, she has to read
   feedback from clients about their holidays.
   Read the questionnaire on the opposite page
   and answer the questions.

   a  Which country did the client visit?
      Slovenia..................................
   b  Which areas did he visit?
      ....................................................
   c  Which hotels did he stay in?
      ....................................................
   d  Did he enjoy his holiday?
      ....................................................

### Did you know ...?

Slovenia is a small country in south-eastern Europe
to the east of Italy. It is one of the six republics that
made up the former Yugoslavia. Much of the land
is mountainous and is very good for walking; the
highest mountain is Mount Triglav (2,863 m) in the
Julian Alps in the north-west. The town of Kranjska
Gora is a popular resort in both summer and winter.
Bled, on the shore of Lake Bled, and Lake
Bohinj also attract many walkers and skiers.

2  **Which of these aspects of the holiday did the
   client particularly like? Tick ✓ one or more of
   the boxes.**
   a  the bedroom at the Vila Orel ☐
   b  the breakfasts at the Vila Orel and the Hotel Bella
      Vista ☐
   c  the picnic lunches at the Vila Orel and the Turist Hotel ☐
   d  the welcome and service at the Turist Hotel and the
      Hotel Bella Vista ☐

3  **Look at the client's two comments about
   the hotels. Circle the correct words in these
   sentences.**
   a  Comment 1 is *positive / negative*.
   b  Comment 2 is mainly *positive / negative*.

4  <u>Underline</u> **the client's criticism in each
   comment.**

For office use AB E6879 22/09 – 01/10

| RM | DR | ACT | CR | RESP |
|----|----|-----|----|----|

**Mr B Drummond CF6 4UE**

## MOUNTAIN TRAVEL POST-HOLIDAY QUESTIONNAIRE

We are constantly working to maintain and improve all aspects of our service. Your comments are vital to us in this effort and are much appreciated. Please use our special FREEPOST address: Mountain Travel Ltd, FREEPOST, York Y03 7BT.

### The Lakes & Julian Alps – a holiday in Slovenia

HOW WOULD YOU DESCRIBE YOUR OVERALL LEVEL OF SATISFACTION WITH YOUR HOLIDAY?

**Please tick as applicable:**

Very satisfactory ✓    Satisfactory ☐
Fairly satisfactory ☐    Unsatisfactory ☐

### ACCOMMODATION

Please rate aspects of each hotel on a scale of 1 to 5, with 5 the highest score.

|  | Vila Orel (Kranjska Gora) | Turist Hotel (Lake Bohinj) | Hotel Bella Vista (Lake Bled) |
|----|----|----|----|
| Bedroom | 5 | 3 | 4 |
| Breakfast | 5 | 4 | 5 |
| Picnic Lunch | 3 | 3 | n/a |
| Welcome & service | 4 | 3 | 3 |
| Hotel Facilities | 4 | 4 | 4 |

**Do you have any other comments about the hotels?**

① We had paid for picnic lunches in both the Vila Orel and the Turist Hotel - every day we got the same boring cheese roll. Would it not be possible for guests to make their own picnic from the breakfast buffet?
② The Vila Orel is very nice indeed. Its location near the river and at the foot of the mountains is something special. My only criticism is that there is no lift - the poor receptionist had to carry my suitcase up two flights of stairs!

### TRAVEL

Please rate aspects of your travel arrangements on a scale of 1 to 5, with 5 as the highest score

**FLIGHTS**    **TRANSFERS**
Adria Airways 4    Taxi Jager 4
    Taxi Pehta 4

Each questionnaire is read by a member of our senior management and all comments are used to improve our holidays. Any negative comments will be particularly scrutinized and shared with hoteliers or other of our partners where appropriate.

Please tick this box only if you wish to receive a reply to the points you have raised on your questionnaire: ☐
You can expect a response within three weeks of your questionnaire arriving with us.

### MANY THANKS FOR COMPLETING THIS QUESTIONNAIRE

5 **What does Mountain Travel claim to do with any negative comments it receives? Tick ✓ one or more of the boxes.**

a They consider any negative comments very carefully. ☐
b They always pass on negative comments to the hotel owners. ☐
c They always let the client know what they have done in response to his or her comment. ☐

6 **What do you think Mountain Travel might do in connection with Mr Drummond's comments?**

7 **Look at some more clients' comments and decide if each one is mainly positive (P) or mainly negative (N). Then think about how Mountain Travel could deal with any negative comments.**

a I understood that the Vila Orel was in Kranjska Gora - but it's 20 minutes' walk from the town. Walking there and back in the dark to the nearest restaurant is not my idea of fun! _N_

b Our holiday was at the end of September, so the hotels were quiet. My friend and I had booked a twin room. However, we each had a large double room in the attic at the Vila Orel. The rooms were wonderful! _____

c It's lovely to have the swimming pools at the Vila Orel and Turist Hotel - and to have them to yourselves! _____

d The Turist Hotel is in a very quiet location off the main road at the far end of the lake. Wouldn't it be possible to stay at the opposite end of the lake - in the village of Bohinj itself? I noticed the Hotel Julija there. It's very near the lake, and there are shops and things! _____

e The Hotel Bella Vista has wonderful gardens and a fantastic location. I don't recommend staying there on Saturday night, however! When we were there, a wedding party went on until five am. The music was incredibly loud and the receptionist didn't want to do anything about it! _____

### Class bonus

Write some positive and negative comments about a hotel you have stayed in. Exchange your comments with a partner. As you read your partner's comments, imagine you are Ivana. Is each comment positive or negative? What – if anything – might you do about the negative comments?

# B Report on questionnaire feedback

1 Ivana's boss has asked her to analyse the feedback from all the holiday questionnaires she received and to write a report on the findings. Skim her report and answer the questions.

a Which holiday is the report about?

----------------------------------------

b What is the main focus of the report?

----------------------------------------

2 Look at the first paragraph. In terms of the report, which is the more important number – 239 or 150?

3 How satisfied were the clients? Choose the correct words to make a sentence.

More than *a quarter / half / three-quarters* were *fairly satisfied / satisfied / very satisfied*.

4 Look at the chart in the report and answer the questions.

a Which aspect of which hotel was the most highly rated?

*the bedrooms at the Hotel*
*Bella Vista (98%)*

b Which aspect of which hotel was the lowest rated?

----------------------------------------

c Which hotel was most highly rated overall?

----------------------------------------

d Which aspect was the most highly rated overall?

----------------------------------------

5 Underline the four most common client criticisms mentioned in Ivana's report.

## The Lakes and Julian Alps: feedback from holiday questionnaires

The Lakes and Julian Alps is one of our most popular holidays – there were 239 bookings during the summer season (a total of 506 clients). However, of the 239 questionnaires which were sent out to clients, only 150 were returned.

**Overall satisfaction** with the holiday was very high. Responses were as follows:

| | |
|---|---|
| very satisfactory | 116 |
| satisfactory | 33 |
| fairly satisfactory | 2* |
| unsatisfactory | 0 |

* Both holidays were spoilt by poor weather. In addition, one group got food poisoning in a restaurant in Kranjska Gora.

**Accommodation**

Clients rate five aspects of each hotel, with a mark from 1 (minimum) to 5 (maximum). The results from 150 questionnaires give a minimum total of 150 and a maximum total of 750. The total mark for each aspect has been converted into a percentage of the maximum possible. For example: a total of 690 out of 750 = 92%. The results are:

| | Vila Orel (Kranjska Gora) | Turist Hotel (Lake Bohinj) | Hotel Bella Vista (Lake Bled) |
|---|---|---|---|
| Bedroom | 92% | 49% | 98% |
| Breakfast | 81% | 77% | 94% |
| Picnic lunch | 47% | 42% | n/a |
| Welcome & service | 81% | 72% | 88% |
| Facilities | 81% | 70% | 88% |

**Aspects of the accommodation that were most criticised in clients' comments were:**

- **Bedrooms at the Turist Hotel** These are a rather dull brown, but the manager assures us that the hotel will be refurbished this winter. In other words, the rooms will be totally redecorated and updated.
- **Picnic lunches provided by the Vila Orel and the Turist Hotel** These were criticised as being plain and boring. A suggestion was made that guests could make up their own picnic from the breakfast buffet. We have spoken to the managers of both hotels about the picnic lunches; whereas the Vila Orel is happy to adopt this scheme, the Turist Hotel would prefer to continue with the existing situation. I suggest that, in future, guests arrange their own lunches. As a result, we would no longer offer pre-payment for lunches as an option. Either guests can come to an arrangement with the hotel concerned, or they can buy lunch while they are out for the day. Eating out in Slovenia is cheap, and there are places to eat everywhere – even on walks in remote areas.
- **Noise from wedding parties at the Hotel Bella Vista** This can be loud enough to keep guests awake at night. Since most of our guests stay at the hotel on Saturday night, the best thing we can do is to warn clients in advance when they phone us to make their booking.
- **Remote location of the Turist Hotel** Several people suggested that a hotel in the village of Bohinj might be preferable to staying at the far end of the lake. However, there is a frequent bus service (every hour) from the Turist Hotel to Bohinj and then on to Bled; furthermore, the village of Bohinj can be noisy at night.

**Transfers**
No criticisms at all!

## Learning tip

Make sure you know the meaning of words and
expressions used to link facts and ideas. This will help
you to understand the meaning of the text and what
the writer is saying. Here are some examples:

giving a reason — *because, since, as*
expressing a contrast — *whereas, otherwise, but,
while, however, although*
expressing a result — *consequently, therefore, as a
result*
rephrasing — *in other words, i.e.*
giving an example — *for example, for instance, e.g.*
adding something — *furthermore, in addition, also*

**6 Answer these questions about Ivana's
responses to the criticisms. (Circle) any linking
words and expressions in the report that help
you answer the questions.**

a When the rooms at the Turist Hotel are refurbished,
what will happen to them?

--------------------------------------------------

b Are both hotels prepared to let guests choose their own
picnic from the breakfast buffet?

--------------------------------------------------

c Why might Mountain Travel stop offering pre-payment
for lunches as an option?

--------------------------------------------------

d Why should Mountain Travel warn people in advance
about the noise from the wedding parties?

--------------------------------------------------

e Does Ivana want to offer a hotel in Bohinj instead of the
Turist Hotel?

--------------------------------------------------

**7 How do you think Ivana's boss will feel when
she reads this report? Will she be pleased
about the feedback?**

### Focus on ...
**linking words**

(Circle) the correct linking word or expression to
complete this extract from the report.

> Several people suggested that a hotel in the village of
> Bohinj might be preferable to staying at the far end of
> the lake. *However / In addition / Consequently*, there
> is a frequent bus service from the Turist Hotel to
> Bohinj and then on to Bled.

Add a linking word or expression to each of these
sentences before adding them to the end of the four
bulleted paragraphs in the report. (The sentences are in
the same order as the paragraphs.)

a ---------------------- , new lighting will be installed in each
room.

b ---------------------- , on the walk from the Turist Hotel
there is a café serving food just below the waterfall.

c ---------------------- , we could offer another hotel as an
alternative to the Hotel Bella Vista for Saturday nights.

d ---------------------- , this alternative would solve one
problem, but create another.

### E✗tra practice

Look at the website www.realholidayreports.com and read
some reviews of other hotels in Kranjska Gora, Bohinj and
Bled. Click on Reports, then link to Eastern Europe, then
Slovenia. Are the reviews positive or negative?

## Can-do checklist

Tick what you can do.

| | Can do | Need more practice |
|---|---|---|
| I can interpret a completed questionnaire. | ✓ | ✓ |
| I can distinguish between comments and suggested action. | | |
| I can understand how writers link facts and ideas. | | |

# Unit 12
# I'm going to apply

Get ready to **read**

○ If you wanted to find a new job, which of the following would you do? Tick ✓ one or more of the boxes.

Look at advertisements in newspapers or in shop windows. ☐
Phone the Human Resources department of a company you'd like to work for. ☐
Visit the website of a company you'd like to work for and look at the vacancies webpage. ☐
Visit recruitment websites. ☐
Register with a recruitment agency. ☐
Speak to friends and family and ask them for help. ☐

○ Have you ever applied for a job? How did you find it? Did you get the job?

-----------------------------------------------------------------------------------------------

○ What are the main steps in getting a new job? Put these steps in the correct order.
  a  You receive a letter inviting you to attend an interview. ☐
  b  You accept the job offer. ☐
  c  You see an advertisement for a job you're interested in. ☐ 1
  d  You receive a letter or a phone call offering you the job. ☐
  e  You send in your CV or you complete an application form. ☐
  f  You attend the interview. ☐

go to Useful language p. 85

## A I've seen an advert

**1  Imagine you are studying in Dublin, Ireland. You see the advertisement on the opposite page. What is it for? Tick ✓ one of the boxes.**

a  a job on the shop floor of a bookshop ☐
b  a job in the mail order department of a bookshop ☐
c  a job in the accounts department of a bookshop ☐

**2  Read the advertisement again and answer as many of these questions as you can.**

a  What is the title of the job?
   *Part-time Administrator*
   ----------------------------------------------

b  Where exactly would you work?

   ----------------------------------------------

c  What would you do?

   ----------------------------------------------

d  How many hours would you work each week?

   ----------------------------------------------

e  What time would you finish work each day?

   ----------------------------------------------

f  How much would you get paid?

   ----------------------------------------------

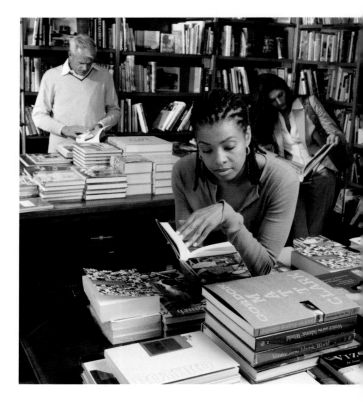

# THE INTERNATIONAL BOOK SHOP
23–25 MEATH ROAD, DUBLIN 4

**VACANCY**
**PART-TIME ADMINISTRATOR**
**20 HRS/WK – MORNINGS**

We have a part-time vacancy in our Mail Order department at The International Book Shop. The shop is the premier international bookshop in Ireland and comprises a large range of books, magazines and newspapers, plus a growing Mail Order business.

Our Mail Order department is expanding rapidly and we are seeking to employ an administrator to handle orders, keep the database up-to-date and carry out general tasks related to customer orders. The role would be offered initially on a part-time basis. The required hours would cover 5 mornings a week with a 9 am start and would include Saturday mornings. There may be the option to become full time.

Applicants must have:
1 ■ Strong data input skills and familiarity with using spreadsheets, databases, email and word processing.
2 ■ Natural enthusiasm and a confident telephone manner.
3 ■ An understanding of the importance of attention to detail and accuracy.
4 ■ A methodical approach to tasks.
5 ■ A willingness to learn in a customer-focused environment.
6 ■ A willingness to take their own initiative.
A foreign language is desirable but not essential.

Deadline for applications: Wednesday 2nd August

To apply, please send in your CV to
Michael O'Grady, Manager, The International Book Shop, 23–25 Meath Road, Dublin 4

**3 Which of the sentences below describe you? Tick ✓ one or more of the boxes.**

a I can make decisions and do things without someone telling me what to do. ☐
b I plan my day's work in an ordered way. ☐
c I am keen to be involved and like talking to people. ☐
d I am motivated and enjoy finding out about new things. ☐
e I am careful to get everything exactly right. ☐

**4 Match the sentences in Exercise 3 with qualities listed in the advertisement. Write the numbers of the bullet points in the boxes.**

a 6 b ☐ c ☐ d ☐ e ☐

**5 You decide to apply for the job. How do you apply for it? When must you apply?**

**6 Pilar, a student in your class, also wants to apply for the job. Look at this part of her CV. Do you think Pilar is suitable for the job? Why? / Why not?**

### Previous employment

**1 Sales assistant  London  3 months**
Main responsibilities: stocking shelves, selling goods, dealing with refunds.
Reasons for leaving: Summer job only – returned to Madrid for commercial course.

**2 Personal Assistant  Madrid  2 years**
Main responsibilities: office administration/ correspondence, accounts and customer service.
Reasons for leaving: The business was sold, and I lost my job.

**3 Tour guide  Madrid  6 months**
Main responsibilities: showing groups of people around the city.
Reasons for leaving: I wanted to come to Dublin to study English.

**Languages** Spanish (mother tongue), English (proficient), French (intermediate)

**7 Would you be interested in this job? Why? / Why not?**

## Class bonus
Think about a job you've had (or one that you would like). What skills and qualities did / would you need for it? Write a list. Don't include the job title. Exchange lists with another person. Try to guess your partner's job.

## E✗tra practice
Look at the job advertisements section of a newspaper from your country. Are any of the advertisements in English? Do any of them mention that English is required? Do any of them mention which skills and qualities are desirable? Cut out an advertisement that interests you.

## B Further to our telephone conversation

**1** You are going to read a letter which uses formal language. First look at the pairs of words in *italics*. Circle the more formal alternative.

a *in* / *within* our company
b your *pay* / *salary* will be
c depends on *completion* / *finishing*
d 10 days' *holiday* / *leave*
e your *proposed* / *suggested* working hours
f *All the best,* / *Yours sincerely,* Michael O'Grady

**2** Read the letter and tick ✓ the correct sentence.

a The letter is telling Pilar that she hasn't got the job at the bookshop. ☐
b The letter is offering Pilar the job at the bookshop. ☐
c The letter is repeating the job offer made over the phone. ☐

---

### The International Book Shop
23–25 Meath Road
Dublin 4

tel: (00353) 1 249241
fax: (00353) 1 790061

Ms Pilar Morientes
76 Cork Place
Dublin 7

14 August 20__

Dear Ms Morientes

Re: Part-time Administrator

Further to our telephone conversation, I am delighted to confirm our offer of employment as Part-time Administrator within our organization.

The position is offered to you at a salary of £8,000 per annum and is subject to successful completion of the 13-week probationary period and receipt of satisfactory references.

1 Your normal working week will total 20 hours. Where it is necessary for you to work in excess of your normal hours, extra payment will be made.
2 Annual leave entitlement starts at 22 days per financial year and increases with service.
3 Your remuneration will be paid by direct credit transfer into a Bank / Building Society Account, on the last Friday of each calendar month.

Please would you confirm acceptance of this offer in writing as soon as possible, together with your proposed commencement date.

In the meantime, may I wish you every success in your future with our company.

Yours sincerely

*Michael O'Grady*

Michael O'Grady
Manager

---

## Learning tip

Most of our everyday correspondence, such as notes and emails, is in informal language. However, on some occasions we receive formal letters. The language used in these is serious and correct, and less like spoken language. One way of understanding the content of a formal letter is to put it into more neutral everyday language.

## Did you know …?

Formal letters end *Yours sincerely* when the sender knows the person he / she is writing to, or knows the name of the person. When the sender doesn't know the name of the recipient, letters begin *Dear Sir or Madam* and end *Yours faithfully*.

**3** Read the letter and find a more formal alternative for these words.

a  work       employment
b  job
c  depends on
d  more than
e  start

**4** Explain these parts of the letter in your own words.

a  Further to our telephone conversation
   We have already spoken on the phone and

b  to confirm our offer

c  £8,000 per annum

d  13-week probationary period

e  Annual leave entitlement

f  22 days per financial year

g  increases with service

h  remuneration

## Focus on …
### the layout of letters

Read these sentences about the layout of formal letters. Are the sentences true (T) or false (F)?

a  The letterhead – the sender's business address, etc. – is at the top of the page. __T__
b  The receiver's name and address are on the right. _____
c  The date is below the receiver's address. _____
d  The subject heading is under the salutation (*Dear* …). _____
e  Formal letters are never typed. _____
f  There is a space between each paragraph. _____
g  There is no space before the first word of each paragraph. _____
h  Letters end with a signature below the typed name and title. _____

Write Pilar's letter of acceptance. In your letter, make sure you:
– thank Michael O'Grady for the offer
– state your preferred start date
– say that you have booked a holiday in October.
Remember to lay out your letter in the correct way.

**5** What does Pilar have to do if she wants the job?

## Can-do checklist

Tick what you can do.

| | Can do | Need more practice |
|---|---|---|
| I can understand a job advertisement. | ✓ | ✓ |
| I can distinguish between formal and informal language. | | |
| I can understand an offer of employment and confirm acceptance. | ✓ | ✓ |

# Unit 13
# I'm off on a trip

## Get ready to read

- Match the industries with the icons.
  - a agriculture [4]
  - b chemicals [ ]
  - c financial and business services [ ]
  - d manufacturing [ ]
  - e petroleum [ ]
  - f tourism [ ]

- What are the main industries in your country or region? Write a list. Use the words above and any others.

------------------------------------------------------------

go to Useful language p. 86

## A Economic structure

1 Youssef, who works for a chemical company in the United States, is going on a business trip to Singapore. He decides to find out about Singapore's Gross Domestic Product – the total value of goods produced and services provided by the country in a year – on a website. Look at these tables from one of the webpages. Which of the tables mention GDP? Tick ✓ one or more of the boxes.

a [ ]    b [ ]    c [ ]    d [ ]

### Learning tip

We don't only read texts. We also read visuals, such as tables, graphs and diagrams. Often these are a more direct way of presenting information than through text. Visuals sometimes have to be read with text, but at other times they stand alone. As with texts, we always read them with a purpose and that is to extract meaning.

## Economic structure of Singapore

a

|  | 2002 | 2003 | 2004 | 2005 |
|---|---|---|---|---|
| GDP at market prices (S$ bn) | 158.4 | 161.5 | 181.7 | 194.4 |
| GDP (US$ bn) | 88.5 | 92.7 | 107.5 | 116.8 |
| Real GDP growth (%) | 4.0 | 2.9 | 8.7 | 6.4 |
| Export of goods (US$ bn) | 140.8 | 161.7 | 201.0 | 232.3 |
| Exchange rate (S$: US$) | 1.79 | 1.74 | 1.69 | 1.66 |
| Population (m) | 4.2 | 4.2 | 4.2 | 4.3 |

b

| Origins of gross domestic product 2005 | % of total |
|---|---|
| Manufacturing | 26.8 |
| Business services | 12.6 |
| Transport & communications | 11.9 |
| Financial services | 10.8 |
| Construction & utilities | 3.6 |
| Others | 34.3 |

c

| Principal exports 2005 | US$ bn |
|---|---|
| Machinery & equipment | 135.2 |
| Petroleum products | 27.6 |
| Chemicals | 26.2 |
| Manufactured goods | 10.5 |
| Food | 2.3 |

d

| Main destinations of exports 2005 | % of total |
|---|---|
| Malaysia | 14.3 |
| US | 11.0 |
| Hong Kong | 10.1 |
| China | 9.3 |
| Japan | 5.9 |
| Thailand | 4.4 |
| South Korea | 3.8 |

**2** **Are these statements about Singapore's GDP true (T) or false (F)?**

a GDP was worth just over 90 billion US dollars in 2002. __F__

b GDP rose by less than three per cent in 2003. ......

c The GDP's rate of growth in 2004 was three times what it was in 2003. ......

d GDP increased by just under 9 billion US dollars in 2005. ......

e The manufacturing sector contributed the most to GDP in 2005. ......

f The transport and communications sector contributed more to GDP in 2005 than the business services sector. ......

g The contribution to GDP of the financial services sector was twice that of the construction and utilities sector in 2005. ......

**3** **Look at tables c and d on the opposite page. (Circle) the correct words in these sentences.**

a The value of chemicals was (more) / less than the value of manufactured goods which were exported in 2005.

b Chemicals were the *third / second* biggest export in 2005.

c More goods were exported to the *US / Hong Kong* in 2005.

d Just *over / under* one tenth of Singapore's exports went to the US in 2005.

**4** **Youssef's company wants to export chemicals to Singapore, so he looks at some import figures. Look at visuals e–g on the webpage on the right. Complete the sentences with these terms.**

| pie chart    bar chart    line graph |

Visual e is a ...............................

Visual f is a ...............................

Visual g is a ...............................

## Did you know ...?

The tiny island state of Singapore, south of Malaysia, is one of the world's most prosperous places. It has one of the busiest ports in the world and is the world's fourth largest foreign exchange trading centre.

**5** **Look again at both webpages and compare the information about imports and exports. (Circle) the correct phrase in each sentence. Sometimes you will need to look at one webpage and sometimes you will need to look at both.**

a In 2005, Singapore imported *more than / (less than) / the same amount as* it exported.

b The value of Singapore's imports between 2002 and 2005 *fell / rose / stayed the same*.

c In 2005, Singapore imported *more chemicals than / fewer chemicals than / the same quantity of chemicals as* it exported.

d In 2005, Singapore spent more on imported manufactured goods than it did on imported *machinery and equipment / food / crude petroleum*.

e In 2005, Singapore imported *more from China than / less from China than / about the same amount from China as* from Japan.

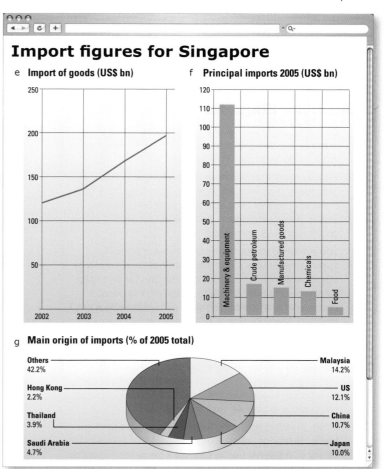

**Import figures for Singapore**

e **Import of goods (US$ bn)**

f **Principal imports 2005 (US$ bn)**

g **Main origin of imports (% of 2005 total)**

Others 42.2% — Malaysia 14.2% — Hong Kong 2.2% — US 12.1% — Thailand 3.9% — China 10.7% — Saudi Arabia 4.7% — Japan 10.0%

## Class bonus

Find out about another country and its exports and imports on the *Economist* website www.economist.com/countries Write some sentences like those in Exercise 5. Exchange your sentences with a partner. Can you choose the correct word in your partner's sentences?

# B Business etiquette

**1** In the United States, there are certain ways of behaving at business meetings that are considered polite. Read this list of business etiquette instructions for the United States. Do people in your country do these things at business meetings? Tick ✓ one or more of the boxes.

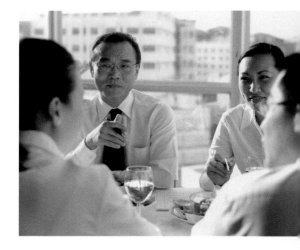

a  Always wear a jacket. ☐
b  Arrive on time. ☐
c  Greet people with 'Good morning / afternoon', or the equivalent. ☐
d  Shake other people's hands firmly as a way of greeting. ☐
e  Look other people in the eye to show interest and respect. ☐

**2** Youssef wants to find out about business etiquette in Singapore, so he reads this webpage. Read it and find out if business people in Singapore do the things in Exercise 1. Write *Y* (yes) or *N* (no).

a <u>N</u>   b ......   c ......   d ......   e ......

File   Edit   View   Favorites   Tools   Help

Address [                                                ] Go   Links »

## Business Etiquette in Singapore

1  Be polite, professional and patient at all times. This leads to the good relationships which you will need in order to do business in Singapore.

2  Bear in mind that business is done more formally in Singapore than in many Western countries, and that there are rules of etiquette that must be followed. Status is very important, and the eldest person in the group is always respected.

3  You will need to plan ahead. Whenever possible, appointments should be made at least two weeks in advance. Nowadays appointments can be arranged by phone or email, although writing to the person concerned is the most formal way to schedule a meeting. Many businesses close during Chinese New Year (late January / early February), so there is no point in even trying to fix a meeting at this time.

4  Make sure you arrive punctually for business meetings. This is a matter of respect. If you are going as a group, make sure you are lined up according to your status. Likewise, wait to be seated.

5  When meeting someone for the first time, and in formal meetings, always use the person's title and family or personal name. Only use personal names or nicknames when you are invited to do so, or when you have known someone for a long time.

6  Handshaking isn't part of Asian culture, so a handshake in Singapore is much softer and lighter to the touch than a Western one. Singaporeans don't understand the significance that Westerners give to a firm handshake.

7  Business cards are exchanged at the beginning of meetings and are always handed out so that the typeface faces the recipient. Protocol demands that you hold the card with both hands and examine it carefully; before putting the card into your card case, smile in order to show that you have noted who the other person is. This is a form of respect to that person and it reflects how the business relationship will be treated. Make sure your own business cards are in perfect condition before you hand them out.

8  Your Singaporean counterparts may not greet you with 'Good morning / afternoon / evening' or 'How are you?' Instead, you may be asked 'Have you eaten?' or 'Where are you going?'

9  Jackets do not normally have to be worn at meetings because of Singapore's hot and humid weather.

10  Before business discussions begin, there is often a period of small talk. Food, tourist attractions, the arts, music, and mutual friends are the safest topics.

11  As a sign of respect, Singaporeans don't always look people in the eye – especially if the person is older or has a higher status. Asian courtesy is very different from Western behaviour in this case, so don't be offended if this happens to you. Similarly, Singaporeans would not disagree with or question someone who is senior in rank.

**3** What reasons does the webpage give for why Singaporeans do or don't follow the customs mentioned in Exercise 1? <u>Underline</u> the information on the webpage.

**4** What should Youssef do when he receives a business card from someone he meets at a meeting in Singapore? Put the steps in order.

a look at the card carefully ☐
b take the card with both hands ☐1☐
c put the card in his card case ☐
d smile at the other person ☐

YIN MÁRKETING PTE LTD

Kelvin Tan
29 Tuas Road #07-21
(65) 6321 9876
ktanyin@singnet.com.sg

**5** Look at the steps in Exercise 4. Is this the way people exchange business cards in your country?

**6** Here are some sentences which could be added to the end of some of the points on the webpage. Match the sentences with the points in the list. Write the numbers in the boxes.

a Take time to learn Asian etiquette, and to develop business contacts. ☐1☐
b People will take their seats in a strict order. ☐
c Wait for your Singaporean counterpart to offer you their hand for a handshake. ☐
d If you are meeting Chinese Singaporeans, you might consider having one side of your card translated into Mandarin. ☐
e You may need to encourage people to ask questions, so always make sure you smile when someone asks a question. ☐

**7** How similar is business etiquette in Singapore to business etiquette in your country? What are the main similarities and differences?

## Focus on ...
### the passive infinitive

Complete these extracts from the webpage.
a there are rules of etiquette that must __be followed__
b appointments should _____ at least two weeks in advance
c appointments can _____ by phone or email

Find and underline five more examples of the passive infinitive in the text.

Complete these sentences with the passive infinitive of the verb in brackets.
d Don't _____ to take off your jacket. (embarrass)
e You have to _____ when to sit down. (tell)
f You may _____ to use personal names. (invite)
g You mustn't _____ before your boss. (introduce)
h You may _____ with a nod rather than a handshake. (greet)
i You will _____ to arrive on time for business meetings. (expect)

## E✗tra practice

Read about business etiquette in your own country on the Internet. The website www.cyborlink.com may be able to help you. Do you agree with everything that you read? Have you learned anything you didn't know?

## Can-do checklist

Tick what you can do.

| | Can do | Need more practice |
|---|---|---|
| I can interpret statistics. | ✓ | ✓ |
| I can interpret charts and graphs. | ✓ | ✓ |
| I can find out about business etiquette in another country. | | |

# Unit 14
## Look it up!

go to Useful language p. 86

### Get ready to read

- Match the beginnings and endings of the sentences.
  - a  You can find facts about a large number of subjects in
  - b  You can look up the meaning of a word in
  - c  You can look up synonyms for certain words in

  a dictionary.
  a thesaurus.
  an encyclopaedia.

- Which dictionary would you use if you wanted to do these things?
  - a  find words to put in a poem or song
  - b  understand some very informal expressions
  - c  find a famous saying to include in a speech
  - d  find translations of words into another language
  - e  read definitions of words

  dictionary of quotations
  bilingual dictionary
  monolingual dictionary
  dictionary of slang
  rhyming dictionary

## A  Alphabetical order

**1** Imagine that you want to find the information below to complete a crossword puzzle. Which books would you use to find the information? Match a–d with the book covers 1–4.

- a  words that mean the same as *follower*  3
- b  the meaning of *brass instrument*  ☐
- c  an idiom containing the word *ground*  ☐
- d  the first names of the actors Laurel and Hardy  ☐

### Learning tip

We use reference books for finding specific pieces of information. Each double page of an alphabetically ordered reference book has two words in bold at the top of the pages. These show the first and last entries on those two pages. Our knowledge of the alphabet helps us to scan the reference book to find the words we are looking for.

**2** You are looking for a–d in Exercise 1. Look at the words below. <u>Underline</u> the words which will be on the pages containing the information you want.

- a  FLY – FOLD          <u>FOLK – FOOD</u>
- b  BOXROOM – BRANCH    BRANCH LINE – BREAK
- c  GREAT – GRIP        GRIPS – GUM
- d  LAUD – LAUSANNE     LAVA – LAWRENCE

**3** Read the reference book entries on the right and find the information in Exercise 1.

**brass** [MUSICAL INSTRUMENTS] /braːs/ *adj* [before noun] (of a musical instrument) made of metal and played by blowing: *The trumpet and trombone are brass instruments.* ○ *He plays in the brass section of the orchestra.*

**Laurel and Hardy**  Stan Laurel (1890–1965) and Oliver Hardy (1892–1957) US film comedians. (Laurel was English-born.) Their films include many short, silent films, *Way Out West* 1937, and *A Chump at Oxford* 1940.

**ground**

**be thin on the ground** *British & Australian* if things or people are thin on the ground, there are not many of them ● *Bears are getting rather thin on the ground in European forests.* ● *I get the impression work is a bit thin on the ground at the moment.*

**follower** *noun* **1** disciple, adherent, partisan, pupil. **2** supporter, enthusiast, devotee, fan, servant, attendant, companion.

**4 Read the webpage on the right about Keyword Search. What can you use this search for? Tick ✓ one of the boxes.**

a  to find a specific book ☐
b  to find all the books on a specific topic ☐
c  both of the above ☐

**5 Should you do the following when you do a Keyword Search? Write Y (yes) or N (no) after each statement.**

a  You should be as exact as possible when you choose your keyword(s). __Y__
b  You should try to use five keywords. _____
c  You should put a space between keywords. _____
d  You should put the subject name first and then the author's name. _____

**6 One of your searches gives you very few results. What could you do to get more?**

------------------------------------------------

## Did you know ...?

The Dewey Decimal System of Classification is used in the UK and the USA to organize library collections. It groups together materials on the same subject by using a special numbering system. It consists of ten general classes, which are then further subdivided. For example, 400 is Language, and 423 is English dictionaries. The system was invented by an American librarian, Melvil Dewey, in the 1870s.

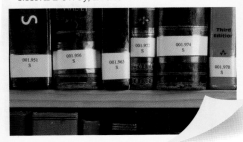

## E ✗ tra practice

Find out if your library uses the Dewey Decimal System of Classification. Use the catalogue to find books on 'reading skills'.

---

**Keyword Search**

- Searching by keyword is a powerful and effective way of finding the information you want from the catalogue.
- The keyword search will work on any combination of words from author, title, series or subject in any order. You can also use the keyword search if you can only partly remember details of an item. For example, to find a book on India written by Dervla Murphy, enter INDIA MURPHY.
- Enter as many keywords as required, separating each keyword with a space. The maximum number of keywords is four.
- You can use the keyword search if you are looking for a particular subject, for example ACID RAIN, STONEHENGE, or CAKE DECORATING.
- Try to make your choice of words as specific as possible. For example, look for STEAM TRAINS not RAILWAYS, or, if looking for a book on roses, use the word ROSE, rather than GARDENING. This will return a smaller list which will meet your requirements more precisely.
- However, if you only type in one word (especially if it is a common one) you may get a long and not very helpful list of matches. On the other hand, too many keywords may narrow your search too far; don't be afraid to experiment!

**7 You want to find items a–f in the library catalogue. Write suitable keywords for each item.**

a  a book by somebody Paton with *cry* and *country* in the title
   _Paton cry country_
   ------------------------------------------------

b  a biography of the Brazilian footballer Ronaldinho
   ------------------------------------------------

c  *The Remains of the Day* – you don't know the author's name
   ------------------------------------------------

d  some information about how to play backgammon
   ------------------------------------------------

e  a book about the history of classical music by Howard Goodall
   ------------------------------------------------

f  a book to help you improve your reading skills
   ------------------------------------------------

**8 Read the webpage below about Class Search. Imagine you want to find the classification number for 'English'. How many ways of finding it does the webpage mention? Underline them.**

**Class Search**

- The library stock is classified according to the Dewey Decimal system, where a number corresponds to a particular subject. If you know the number associated with the subject in which you are interested, you can search for all books with that classification number. This is a good way to search for books on your chosen topic if you know the number. Library staff can help you find the right number, or, if you know of another book on the same subject, you can see what class number it has been given, and use that number in your search. For example: type the class number 001.6 for books about computing, or type 001 for all class numbers starting with 001. Then press the Return key.

**9 You are at a library in Oxfordshire. What kind of books would you look for in the catalogue?**

## B 4.50 from Paddington

### Learning tip

Reading whole articles, stories and books is a good way to improve your extensive reading skills so that reading for study becomes easier.

When you go to a bookshop or library, choose books that you are interested in. Skim two or three pages and make sure there are not too many new words (a maximum of ten per page). If there are more, you won't be able to work out their meaning from the other words in the text. Direct speech breaks up the text and is generally easier than narrative or descriptive writing.

When you start reading, don't stop in the middle of a sentence or paragraph and go back – continue until the end of a page or chapter.

1 **Look at the front and back cover of this book and read the blurb (the description of the book). Then answer the questions.**

   a  Who is the book by? _____
   b  What is it about? _____
   c  Is there a film version of this book?

   _____

2 **What do you know about the author? Have you read any of her books in your own language? Guess the missing numbers in these sentences.**

   a  She wrote _____ crime novels and _____ plays.
   b  Her books have been translated into _____ languages.
   c  More than _____ of her books have been sold in total.

3 **Now read part of the introduction to the book and check your answers to Exercise 2.**

> Agatha Christie is known throughout the world as the Queen of Crime. Her books have sold over a billion copies in English with another billion in 100 foreign languages. She is the most widely published author of all time and in any language, outsold only by the Bible and Shakespeare. She is the author of 80 crime novels and short story collections, 19 plays, and six novels written under the name of Mary Westmacott.

4 **Read the extract from the book on the opposite page. Do you think this extract is from near the beginning or near the end of the story?**

   _____

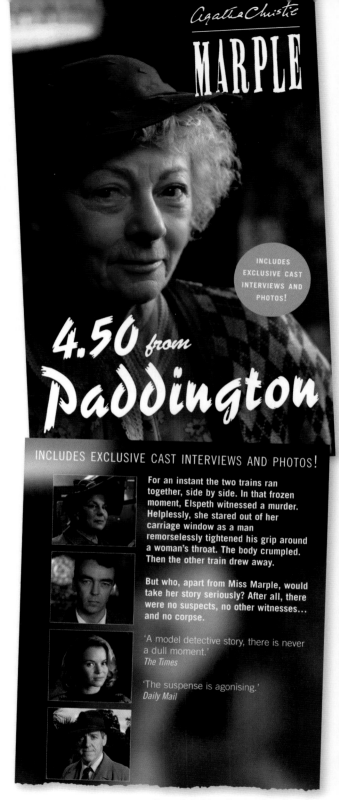

INCLUDES EXCLUSIVE CAST INTERVIEWS AND PHOTOS!

For an instant the two trains ran together, side by side. In that frozen moment, Elspeth witnessed a murder. Helplessly, she stared out of her carriage window as a man remorselessly tightened his grip around a woman's throat. The body crumpled. Then the other train drew away.

But who, apart from Miss Marple, would take her story seriously? After all, there were no suspects, no other witnesses... and no corpse.

'A model detective story, there is never a dull moment.'
*The Times*

'The suspense is agonising.'
*Daily Mail*

5 **The name 'Mrs McGillicuddy' isn't on the back cover of the book. Look at the back cover again and circle Mrs McGillicuddy's first name.**

6 **Does the ticket collector think Mrs McGillicuddy is telling the truth? Underline the parts of the text that help you decide.**

The door of her compartment was drawn back and a ticket collector said, 'Ticket, please'.

Mrs McGillicuddy turned to him with vehemence.

'A woman has been strangled,' she said. 'In a train that has just passed. I saw it.'

The ticket collector looked at her doubtfully.

'I beg your pardon, madam?'

'A man strangled a woman! In a train. I saw it – through there.' She pointed to the window.

The ticket collector looked extremely doubtful.

'Strangled?' he said disbelievingly.

'Yes, *strangled*! I saw it, I tell you. You must *do* something at once!'

The ticket collector coughed apologetically.

'You don't think, madam, that you may have had a little nap and – er –' he broke off tactfully.

'I have had a nap, but if you think this was a dream, you're quite wrong. I *saw* it, I tell you.'

The ticket collector's eyes dropped to the open magazine lying on the seat. On the exposed page was a girl being strangled whilst a man with a revolver threatened the pair from an open doorway.

He said persuasively: 'Now don't you think, madam, that you'd been reading an exciting story, and that you just dropped off, and awaking a little confused –'

Mrs McGillicuddy interrupted him.

'I *saw* it,' she said. 'I was as wide awake as you are. And I looked out of the window into the window of the train alongside, and a man was strangling a woman. And what I want to know is, what are you going to do about it?'

'Well – madam –'

'You're going to do *something*, I suppose?'

The ticket collector sighed reluctantly and glanced at his watch.

'We shall be in Brackhampton in exactly seven minutes. I'll report what you've told me. In what direction was the train you mention going?'

'This direction, of course. You don't suppose I'd have been able to see this if a train had flashed past going in the other direction?'

The ticket collector looked as though he thought Mrs McGillicuddy was quite capable of seeing anything anywhere as the fancy took her. But he remained polite.

'You can rely on me, madam,' he said. 'I will report your statement. Perhaps I might have your name and address – just in case …'

**7 Do you think you might be interested in reading this book? Why? / Why not?**

## Focus on …
### adverbs

Find the words *doubtfully* and *disbelievingly* in the extract and complete these sentences.

a  The ............................................... doubtfully.

b  ............................................... disbelievingly.

These words are adverbs and they describe how someone – in this case, the ticket collector – did something.

Find four more adverbs that describe the ticket collector's actions. What did he do, and how did he do it? Write the verb and the adverb.

c  The ticket collector ...............................................

d  he ...............................................

e  He ...............................................

f  The ticket collector ...............................................

Complete these sentences with the six adverbs from sentences a–f.

g  'Is he really an astronaut?' she asked _disbelievingly_ .

h  The waitress smiled ............................................... as she said that there was no soup.

i  I didn't want to stay late and do the extra work, but in the end I agreed ............................................... .

j  John told us his views and he spoke very ............................................... .

k  'I think you might look better in the blue sweater,' she suggested ............................................... .

l  'I might be able to help you tomorrow, but I'm not sure,' he said ............................................... .

## Class bonus

Work with a partner. One of you is the ticket collector and the other is Mrs McGillicuddy. Read aloud your conversation. (Don't read out the narrative. Only read the direct speech.)

## Can-do checklist

Tick what you can do.

| | Can do | Need more practice |
|---|---|---|
| I can understand instructions in a library catalogue. | ✓ | ✓ |
| I can understand what a novel is about from the blurb. | ✓ | ✓ |
| I can read fiction without worrying about difficult language. | ✓ | ✓ |

# Unit 16
# Read about reading

go to Useful language p. 86

## Get ready to read

○ Answer these questions.
What kinds of things have you read today? _____
How many languages do you read regularly? _____
What kinds of things do you read in English? _____
What sort of difficulties do you have when you read in English? _____

○ Think about these questions.

How important is reading in our everyday lives?

What kinds of reading do we do?

How do we read?

○ In this unit, you are going to read extracts from the entry for *Reading* in an encyclopaedia. This entry describes reading in your first language. Do you think the extracts will help you to answer the questions above?

## A Kinds of reading

1 **Look at the statements below about reading. Do you agree with them? Tick ✓ the boxes.**

|   |   | I agree. | I disagree. | I don't know. |
|---|---|---|---|---|
| a | Reading is the act of getting meaning from printed or written words. | | | |
| b | People may read hundreds or thousands of words a day without even looking at a book, newspaper or magazine. | | | |
| c | In the simplest sense, reading means recognizing letters and groups of letters as symbols that stand for particular sounds. | | | |
| d | In most cases, the teaching of reading stresses certain skills, such as word recognition, vocabulary development, and comprehension (understanding of reading matter). | | | |

2 **The statements in Exercise 1 are the first sentences of the first four paragraphs of the encyclopaedia entry for *Reading*. Here is the rest of one of the paragraphs. Which paragraph (a–d) is it from?**

It is basic to learning and one of the most important skills in everyday life. Reading provides the key to all kinds of information. It enables us to learn how to build or fix things, to enjoy stories, to discover what other people believe, and to develop ideas and beliefs of our own.

## Learning tip

When we read a long text for the first time, we usually skim it in order to find out the general meaning and to identify the parts which we want to read in detail. The most important parts of the text are the first paragraph, which introduces the overall topic, and the first sentence of each of the other paragraphs. This sentence usually introduces the topic of the paragraph.

**3** Read the extract from the entry on the right and <u>underline</u> the most important points.

**4** Are any of the ideas in the extract new to you? Which ones?

**5** Which of the three reading styles – recreational, study-type, survey – have you used to read this extract?

**6** Read the extract again. (Circle) the correct phrases so that the sentences are true.

a Older readers often understand a text more easily because they know more *about reading techniques /* (*information*) than younger readers.

b Good readers use different reading techniques for different *subjects / types of text*.

c Often when we reread part of a story we do this because we *like / can't believe* it.

d When we do study-type reading, we try to *find just the main ideas / link the main ideas together*.

e With survey reading, we read *everything / only some parts* carefully.

f Beginners find reading easier if the text uses language that *they know / is new*.

**7** Does the text describe your experiences as a reader of your own language and of other languages?

### Kinds of reading

People differ in reading ability. For example, those who have been reading a long time tend to understand what they have read more quickly and more automatically than do new readers. In addition, older readers bring more background experiences to their reading. They can use their experiences to fill in important information that is not clearly stated in the text.

A good reader uses various reading techniques. The technique depends on the type and difficulty of the material, the purpose for reading it, and the reader's own language development and familiarity with the subject.

Reading can be classified into three main kinds: (1) recreational reading, (2) study-type reading, and (3) survey reading. Good readers can easily shift from one kind to another, depending on their purpose for reading and on the material itself.

**Recreational reading** can provide hour after hour of enjoyment. When reading a story purely for pleasure, most people read at a relaxed, uneven speed. They may skim through a tale until they come to a scene, a description, or even a phrase that is especially pleasing or satisfying. That portion may be read slowly and then reread to be enjoyed, appreciated, or considered.

**Study-type reading** usually requires the reader to pay close attention to the text. A good reader looks for significant ideas and details. The reader then tries to understand how those ideas and details relate to one another and how they fit into the general topic. Reading speed tends to be slower the first time study-type material is read, and the reader may need to reread portions of the text to understand it fully. Reading speed may be much faster when the material is reviewed.

**Survey reading** involves covering a large amount of text to get a general idea of its content. In such cases, the person may first skim the material to understand the main point. The reader may then look for details that reinforce or illustrate that point. The person may then read some sections carefully to make sure that the desired information has been found.

**Shifting among kinds of reading**. Most people use different reading techniques for different reading situations. For example, a mystery enjoyed simply for entertainment may be read rapidly. But a classic Russian novel may call for slow, careful reading. Technical texts that could lead to job advancement or that tell how to fix something usually require thoughtful reading.

Good readers can easily shift from one kind of reading to another. For instance, a student collecting information to write a paper might begin surveying articles to see if they fit the topic. One article may lead the student to consider changing the topic, and so the article is studied thoroughly and another topic chosen. While surveying for the new topic, the student looks for information to create an outline. During the survey reading, the student may see an entertaining article and read it for pleasure.

Reading flexibility improves with experience. Beginners may tend to read everything somewhat awkwardly, advancing slowly word by word because they doubt their ability to recognize words. By reading materials that follow their own language patterns – that is, familiar words and sentences they use – even beginning readers can read with both speed and understanding. In time, they learn that different reading materials make different demands on their abilities.

**8** What advice would you give to someone who wanted to improve their reading?

### E✗tra practice

Look at the texts you have already read in this book. Decide which reading styles you used with each one.

# B How we read

**1** Read another extract from the encyclopaedia entry for *Reading*. This extract deals with these three topics. Put them in the order in which they appear in the text.

  a  the importance of memory in reading ☐
  b  the physical process of reading ☐
  c  how to deal with unfamiliar words ☐

**2** Think about the topics in Exercise 1. Skim the extract and decide which paragraphs you need to read more carefully to find out about each topic.

Topic a ------------------------------------------
Topic b ------------------------------------------
Topic c ------------------------------------------

**3** Read the paragraphs about the physical process of reading. As you read, think about the words in *italics*. Why are they in *italics*? Tick ✓ one of the boxes.

  a  They are technical terms that are probably unfamiliar to most readers. ☐
  b  They are important and difficult words that the reader has to understand. ☐
  c  They are words that are explained in the paragraph. ☐
  d  More than one of the above. ☐
  e  All of the above. ☐

## Did you know ...?

*Italic* type takes its name from Italy. It is characteristic of the typefaces used by early Italian printers, such as the Aldine Press of Venice. Originally italic type was used for entire texts; it was first used as a secondary typeface in the 18th century.

## How we read

[1] Reading depends first on our *perceiving* (seeing and recognizing) written or printed letters and words. We must then be able to comprehend what we perceive.

[2] **Perceiving reading matter.** The process of reading begins as our eyes see *visual stimuli* – that is, the printed or written symbols that make up what is to be read. Eye movements across the symbols capture the stimuli. Eye movements called *saccadic movements* take place as our eyes move across a page, pausing briefly to take in groups of words. As our eyes move across a line, they alternatively pause and move on. The pauses are called *fixations*. Another type of eye movement, *regression*, occurs when our eyes shift back to reread a word or group of words. To move from one line to the next, our eyes use a movement called a *return sweep*. However, good readers are unaware of their eye movements as they read.

[3] **Comprehending what is perceived.** Reading involves far more than simply seeing visual stimuli. You must first choose a particular piece to satisfy some purpose. That purpose not only determines the selection of the text but also helps you decide which experiences and reading skills to use to comprehend the material. Your purpose may also suggest how you might use any new knowledge or understanding that you gain from the material.

[4] While reading, you draw on numerous ideas and feelings stored in your memory. Those ideas and feelings make up your *background*. You also rely on verbal memory – that is, an understanding of how words come together and form more complex ideas.

[5] Your background and verbal memory change and grow with each reading experience. Information in new material blends with your past experiences and may correct misunderstandings, provide fresh knowledge, broaden interests, or help solve problems.

[6] In many cases, readers lack the background and verbal memory needed to comprehend a text quickly and easily. Such readers may use techniques called *word-recognition strategies*. The more experienced a reader becomes, the more automatically the reader applies these strategies to comprehend unfamiliar words.

[7] Readers can use several general types of word-recognition strategies. For example, a reader who does not know the meaning of a particular word may look for *context clues* in the surrounding text. These clues may be either *semantic* or *syntactic*. When using semantic clues, the reader tries to relate the word to other information or illustrations in the material. Semantic clues include comparisons and contrasts, definitions, descriptions, and the placement of new words near familiar words that help explain their meaning. A reader may also rely on syntactic clues – that is, the word's position and grammatical use in the text. For example, deciding whether a word is functioning as a noun, verb, adjective, or adverb can help a reader figure out its meaning.

[8] In a word-recognition strategy called *structural analysis*, a reader uses clues within the word itself to guess what the word means. The reader relies on knowledge of the meanings of prefixes, suffixes, *roots* (word bases), compound words, and endings such as ed and ing, and of how they are combined. For example, the adverb *undoubtedly* has the prefix *un*, the root *doubt*, ending *ed*, and the suffix *ly*. Knowing the meanings of the parts of the word leads the reader to decide that the word means *without doubt*. And without doubt the best way for readers to add such knowledge to verbal memory is to encounter words made of those parts in text they find meaningful, and to use the words in conversation and writing.

## Class bonus

Choose either the topic of 'the importance of memory' or 'how to deal with unfamiliar words'. Work with someone who has chosen the same topic and read the paragraphs about it again. Help each other with any difficulties in the text.

**4** Read about topics a and c from Exercise 1 – the importance of memory in reading, and how to deal with unfamiliar words. Are these sentences true (T) or false (F)?

a Our verbal memory only helps us to understand verbs. __F__
b You can improve your background and verbal memory by reading more. ......
c Good readers don't need to use word-recognition strategies. ......
d Other words in the text can help us understand an unfamiliar word. ......
e Structural analysis is a way of examining the different parts of a word to understand its meaning. ......

**5** Which of the three word-recognition strategies – semantic context clues, syntactic context clues, structural analysis – have you used to read this text?

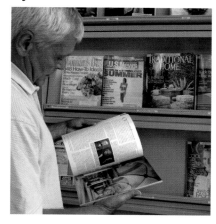

**6** Think of a time when you had difficulty reading something in English or in your own language. Why was it difficult? Did you lack the background or the verbal memory?

**7** What advice would you give to someone who wanted to improve their reading?

## Focus on ...
### prefixes and suffixes

Prefixes and suffixes are groups of letters which are added to words to make new words. In this extract, the verb *read* appears with the prefix *re* (*reread*) and the suffix *ing* (*reading*). A prefix has its own meaning, which becomes part of the meaning of the new word.

A suffix can change the word class of a word, e.g. *comfort* (noun), *comfortable* (adjective), make a word plural (*word*, *words*), or change the tense of a verb (*need*, *needed*).

Add prefixes or suffixes to make words in the extract.
a ...........move _ments_... (paragraph 2)
b ...........aware........... (paragraph 2)
c ...........select........... (paragraph 3)
d ...........inform........... (paragraph 5)
e ...........understand........... (paragraph 5)
f ...........know........... (paragraph 5)

Now complete these sentences. Use the words in a–f above but with different prefixes or suffixes. You might need to use your dictionary.
g It is impossible to remain ____unmoved____ by some of the awful stories in the news.
h Environmental ................... has increased dramatically over the past decade.
i He's very ................... about the people he spends time with.
j It is believed that an ................... has given the police the names of three of the gang.
k It's ................... that he's angry – his car was badly damaged.
l Ask Ahmed about the Pyramids. He's very ................... about Egyptian history.

## Can-do checklist

Tick what you can do.

| | Can do | Need more practice |
|---|---|---|
| I can skim a text and identify the main points. | ✔ | ✔ |
| I can identify the topic of each paragraph within a text. | | |
| I can relate what I have read to my own experiences. | | |

# Review 2
## Units 9–16

**A  Are these statements true (T) or false (F)?**

1  You can often use other words in the text to work out the meaning of an unknown word. ...... (Unit 9)
2  If an email is sent to someone else and you are copied in, you don't need to read the email. ...... (Unit 10)
3  Writers use linking words and expressions to show the relationships between different ideas in a text. ...... (Unit 11)
4  Formal letters may contain language which we don't use in our everyday lives. ...... (Unit 12)
5  Charts and graphs can present figures more directly than a piece of text. ...... (Unit 13)
6  We skim reference books in order to find what we are looking for. ...... (Unit 14)
7  It is easier to work out the meaning of unknown words from context if there are not too many of them on the page. ...... (Unit 15)
8  Reading the first sentence of each paragraph will not help you to get a general idea of what the text is about. ...... (Unit 16)

**B  Now read the *Learning tips* for Units 9–16 on pages 89–91. Do you want to change any of your answers in Exercise A?**

**C  Skim Texts A–D on the opposite page. What is each text, or where does it come from? Use the words in the list.**

| an email   a leaflet   a letter   a novel   a questionnaire |
| a non-fiction book   a report   a webpage |

  9  Text A  ..............................
10  Text B  ..............................
11  Text C  ..............................
12  Text D  ..............................

**D  Read Text A and find the following words. Match the words with descriptions a–c. Write the letters in the boxes.**

13  blog ☐
14  computer ☐
15  hardware ☐
16  email ☐
17  virus ☐

a  a new word
b  a word whose original meaning is still in use and which also has a new meaning
c  a word whose original meaning is no longer in use, but which now has a new meaning

**E  Read Text B. Which of this information does Linda provide? (✓ = information given, ✗ = information not given)**

18  the taxi company that Sofia should contact ☐
19  where Linda is flying to ☐
20  when the taxi should pick her up ☐
21  where it should pick her up from ☐
22  when she is coming back ☐

**F  Read Text C. Choose the five adjectives which best describe Linnet Ridgeway. Write the letters in the boxes in alphabetical order.**

23 ☐   24 ☐   25 ☐   26 ☐   27 ☐

a  blonde
b  confident
c  elderly
d  elegant
e  famous
f  friendly
g  good-looking
h  intelligent
i  rich
j  shy

**G  Look at the tables in Text D. They show the top six exporters and importers of watches and clocks between 2002 and 2005. Circle the correct words in the sentences.**

28  The value of Switzerland's exports rose by the greatest amount in *2003 / 2004 / 2005*.
29  The total value of Germany's exports was *the same as / less than / more than* the total value of its imports during this four-year period.
30  The value of Hong Kong's exports rose *by the same amount as / less than / more than* the value of its imports in this period.
31  Italy was the fifth highest importer in *one / two / three* of the years.
32  From its position in exports in 2004, Japan *rose a position / dropped a position / stayed in the same position* in 2005.

Text A

# Wanted: A computer, female aged 18–25

Over the last 30 years, the biggest source of neologisms or new words in English has probably been computing. *Internet* first appeared in 1986, for instance, and has since become an everyday word for many people. *Email* first appeared in 1982 and *blog* in 1998.

New ideas are not only expressed by coining words. Even more common is adding fresh meanings to existing words. Still within the computing field, the words *mouse*, *hardware*, *program*, *virus* and *monitor* have all taken on new meanings in the last 50 years, but they continue to be used with their original senses – a mouse is still a small rodent as well as a computing device.

When a new meaning is added, however, the original sense is not always retained. A *computer* used to be a role involving lots of addition and subtraction. With the introduction of calculators and machine computers, there was no longer any need for human computers, and the job-related meaning of the word became obsolete. Nowadays, a 1930s recruitment advert such as the one in the title of this chapter sounds very strange.

Text B

Delete  Reply  Reply All  Forward  Print

Hi Sofia

Do you think you could book me a taxi for Monday morning? My flight leaves at 9.40 am, so I'd better be at the airport at 7.40 at the latest. Can you ask the taxi company to confirm what time they'll pick me up (they should know how long it'll take at that time of day from Debden to Luton Airport). My address is Raymond's Cottage (it's the white house on the main street opposite the newsagent's) and the phone number is (01779) 54481. Thanks!
Linda

PS I won't need a return taxi. My husband's going to pick me up on Friday evening.

Text C

LINNET RIDGEWAY!

"That's *Her*!" said Mr. Burnaby, the landlord of the Three Crowns.

He nudged his companion.

The two men stared with round bucolic eyes and slightly open mouths.

A big scarlet Rolls Royce had just stopped in front of the local post office.

A girl jumped out, a girl without a hat and wearing a frock that looked (but only looked) simple. A girl with golden hair and straight autocratic features – a girl with a lovely shape – a girl such as was seldom seen in Malton-under-Wode.

With a quick imperative step she passed into the post office.

"That's her!" said Mr. Burnaby again. And he went on in a low awed voice. "Millions she's got. ... Going to spend thousands on the place. Swimming pools there's going to be, and Italian gardens and a ballroom and half of the house pulled down and rebuilt ..."

"She'll bring money into the town," said his friend.

He was a lean, seedy-looking man. His tone was envious and grudging.

Mr. Burnaby agreed.

"Yes, it's a great thing for Malton-under-Wode. A great thing it is."

Text D

**Watches and clocks: exports 2002–2005 (US$ bn)**

|  | 2002 | 2003 | 2004 | 2005 |
|---|---|---|---|---|
| Switzerland | 6.8 | 7.6 | 8.9 | 9.9 |
| Hong Kong* | 4.9 | 5.4 | 5.9 | 5.9 |
| China | 1.7 | 1.9 | 2.1 | 2.0 |
| Germany | 0.7 | 0.9 | 1.0 | 1.1 |
| Japan | 1.0 | 1.0 | 1.1 | 0.9 |
| France | 0.6 | 0.7 | 0.7 | 0.8 |

**Watches and clocks: imports 2002–2005 (US$ bn)**

|  | 2002 | 2003 | 2004 | 2005 |
|---|---|---|---|---|
| Hong Kong* | 3.8 | 4.1 | 4.6 | 4.7 |
| United States | 3.3 | 3.7 | 3.9 | 4.0 |
| Japan | 1.7 | 1.8 | 2.1 | 2.2 |
| Italy | 0.9 | 1.0 | 1.2 | 1.2 |
| Switzerland | 1.0 | 1.0 | 1.2 | 1.2 |
| Germany | 0.9 | 1.1 | 1.2 | 1.2 |

*Hong Kong Special Administrative Region of China

## H Skim this text from a Health and Safety leaflet.

33 Who is the text for? Tick ✓ one of the boxes.
a people who work in hospitals ☐
b people who work in shops ☐
c people who work in schools ☐

34 What dangers does the text mention? Tick ✓ one of the boxes.
a dangers inside a building ☐
b dangers outside a building ☐
c dangers both inside and outside a building ☐

# Slips, trips and falls are a danger to you and your customers

Pay special attention to these trouble spots

## Floors

- Watch out for loose carpeting, floorboards and tiles.
- Also watch out for cracked, loose or crumbling surfaces.
- Keep the floor clear. Any small thing, even a pen, can cause a fall.

Damaged areas should be reported to your manager as soon as possible.

### Stairs, aisles and walkways

Don't store materials on the stairs or in passageways. Keep passageways free of boxes, rubbish bins and other obstacles. (If an object is in the way, move it or walk around it. Avoid climbing over it.)

### Hidden steps

When turning a corner or stepping outside, look out for steps that may not be obvious. Make sure others are aware of any hidden steps.

## Spills and other wet areas

It only takes a small puddle for a serious accident to happen. Clean up spills and moisture from rain, snow or other substances immediately and place a sign to warn others of the danger.

# Other slip, trip and fall hazards

### Electrical leads

Don't run leads across aisles or under carpets. (This is both a fire and tripping hazard.) And don't use adaptors. If extension leads must be used, make sure they are close to the wall, where people cannot walk or trip over them.

## Icy spots

Walk slowly on any icy surface. Inform your manager of any outside areas where sand or grit is needed.

## Lighting

Make sure customers and colleagues can see where they're going. Report faulty lighting promptly. Use the emergency lighting where necessary and ensure it is in working order by regular testing.

### General tips for preventing falls

- Be alert. Watch where you are going and what you're doing. Watch out for hazards that others might miss.
- Place warning signs or barriers around areas that may be slippery or otherwise dangerous.
- Whether you're working at heights or on the ground, be sure to follow all safety rules. Only use equipment that you've been trained and authorised to use.
- Don't take chances. Avoid tasks that are beyond your ability.

**I** **Find the following words in the text and complete the exercise.**

35  *floors*
    Find three words for different types of floor surface.
    _____

36  *damaged areas*
    Find three adjectives which describe how floors can be damaged.
    _____

37  *obstacle*
    Write a definition of this word using other words from the paragraph.
    _____

38  *obstacles*
    Find two examples of obstacles.
    _____

39  *hidden steps*
    Find a word with the opposite meaning of *hidden*.
    _____

40  *wet areas*
    Find three words for types of wet area.
    _____

41  *electrical lead*
    Find another example of an electrical item.
    _____

42  *faulty lighting*
    Find a phrase with the opposite meaning of *faulty*.
    _____

**J** **Complete these sentences with an example from the text.**

43  You might slip _____
44  You might trip _____
45  You might fall _____

**K** **Kasia works in a shop. The other day she slipped and fell at work. Now she is now looking on her union's website for the answers to some questions. Read the webpage on the right and circle the answers to her questions.**

46  Should there be a qualified first-aid person in all shops and offices?
    yes   no

47  Should the person who looks after the first aid box be a qualified first-aider?
    yes   no

48  Do I have to report my accident in the accident book?
    yes   no

49  Can my boss write a different account of the accident?
    yes   no

**L** **Find verbs in the Answers on the webpage which mean the following.**

50  says _____
51  make sure _____
52  officially choose (someone) _____
53  write down for the future _____
54  experience or have _____
55  tell _____

**❓ Question**

Should first aid be provided in my workplace?

**◻ Short Answer**

Yes, it should. Your employer has to provide adequate first aid for their staff.

**▤ Long Answer**

Regulation 3 of the Health and Safety (First Aid) Regulations 1981 states: 'An employer shall provide, or ensure that there are provided, such equipment and facilities as are adequate and appropriate in the circumstances for enabling first aid to be rendered to his employees if they are injured or become ill at work.

The level of provision will depend on the level of risk and the numbers of employees in the workplace. Guidance states that low risk workplaces like shops or offices should have qualified first-aiders when the number of staff is greater than 50. Otherwise there should be an "appointed person" who has responsibility for keeping the first aid box and calling an ambulance if it is needed. Download our Guide to First Aid for more information.

**❓ Question**

Can my employer stop me putting entries into the accident book?

**◻ Short Answer**

No, they can't. The accident book is there for anyone to make an entry. They can nominate someone to do it for you, but that person must write down what you say.

**▤ Long Answer**

The Social Security Regulations 1979 requires that injuries and diseases are reported and that is why there is an Accident book or a similar means of reporting. An employer might get someone to do this on your behalf for the sake of consistency, but they must record exactly what you say to them. If the employer does not agree with your version of the facts, then he can enter that in the relevant section of the report. If you encounter any problems, then you should inform your safety rep immediately.

# Appendix 1
# Useful language

This section contains a list of words which are important for carrying out the reading exercises for each unit. You can use the list in three ways.

1 You can look at the list before you begin the unit and make sure that you understand the meaning of the words by looking them up in a dictionary.
2 You can look at the list before you begin the unit, but try and work out the meaning of the words when you meet them in the unit.
3 You can look at the list when you have completed the unit and check that you understand the words.

When you start using the book, you may prefer to use the list in the first way. However, you will find each word in one of the texts, and the context – the words around the unknown word – will help you to work out its meaning. As you develop your reading skills, you will probably realize that it is not necessary to look at the list before you begin the unit. You may already know some of the words; you will be able to work out others from the text or the task.

Each list is a record of the vocabulary of the unit. You can use it as a checklist when you have completed the unit. There is space after each word to write a translation in your own language or an English expression using the word. Mark each word that you understand and can use with a highlighter pen.

There is also space below the wordlist for you to write other words from the unit which are important to you. Look at *Appendix 3* for ideas on what to record for each word.

## Unit 1
### Reading A
aubergine *noun* ------------------------------------------------------
garlic *noun* ------------------------------------------------------------
(green) pepper *noun* -----------------------------------------------
olive *noun* --------------------------------------------------------------
basil *noun* ---------------------------------------------------------------
pine nut *noun* --------------------------------------------------------
cocoa powder *noun* -------------------------------------------------
------------------------------------------------------------------------------
------------------------------------------------------------------------------
------------------------------------------------------------------------------

### Reading B
peppercorn *noun* ----------------------------------------------------
coffee bean *noun* ---------------------------------------------------
coffee filter *noun* --------------------------------------------------
------------------------------------------------------------------------------
------------------------------------------------------------------------------
------------------------------------------------------------------------------

## Unit 2
### Reading A
voucher *noun* ---------------------------------------------------------
remark *noun* ----------------------------------------------------------
terms and conditions *noun* ---------------------------------------
available *adjective* --------------------------------------------------
fee *noun* -----------------------------------------------------------------
(bodily) injury *noun* -----------------------------------------------
coverage *noun* -------------------------------------------------------
in effect *expression* ------------------------------------------------
surcharge *noun* ------------------------------------------------------
waiver *noun* -----------------------------------------------------------
collision *noun* --------------------------------------------------------
specified (amount) *adjective* ------------------------------------
theft *noun* --------------------------------------------------------------
------------------------------------------------------------------------------
------------------------------------------------------------------------------
------------------------------------------------------------------------------

### Reading B
in compliance with *expression* -----------------------------------
in accordance with *expression* -----------------------------------
------------------------------------------------------------------------------
------------------------------------------------------------------------------
------------------------------------------------------------------------------

# Unit**3**
## Reading A
let *verb* _____
excluding *preposition* _____
professional *adjective* _____
furnished *adjective* _____
modern conveniences *noun* _____
reference *noun* _____
all inclusive *expression* _____
deposit *noun* _____
_____
_____
_____

## Reading B
tenancy *noun* _____
witness *noun* _____
tenant *noun* _____
landlord *noun* _____
property *noun* _____
term *noun* _____
rent *noun* _____
_____
_____
_____
_____

# Unit**4**
## Reading A
baggage *noun* _____
allowance *noun* _____
dimension *noun* _____
excess (baggage) *adjective* _____
overweight *adjective* _____
oversized *adjective* _____
_____
_____
_____

## Reading B
missing (items) *adjective* _____
trace *verb* _____
delayed (bags) *adjective* _____
destination *noun* _____
boarding card *noun* _____
baggage check label *noun* _____
_____
_____
_____

# Unit**5**
## Reading A
mail *noun* _____
perishable *adjective* _____
postcode *noun* _____
packet *noun* _____
signature *noun* _____
evidence *noun* _____
on your behalf *expression* _____
proof *noun* _____
redeliver *verb* _____
_____
_____
_____

## Reading B
interrupt *verb* _____
guidance *noun* _____
restore *verb* _____
stop valve *noun* _____
_____
_____
_____

# Unit**6**
## Reading A
bed and breakfast *noun* _____
spectacular *adjective* _____
en-suite *adjective* _____
excursion *noun* _____
sanctuary *noun* _____
proprietor *noun* _____
_____
_____
_____

## Reading B
tariff *noun* _____
settle *verb* _____
legally binding *expression* _____
liable *adjective* _____
insure *verb* _____
cancellation *noun* _____
ensure *verb* _____
_____
_____
_____

# Unit 7

**Reading A**

insider *noun* .....................................................................

congregate *verb* ...............................................................

dispersed *adjective* ..........................................................

impeccable *adjective* ........................................................

top-notch *adjective* ..........................................................

perspective *noun* ..............................................................

dossier *noun* ......................................................................

tack on *verb* ......................................................................

adrenalin *noun* ..................................................................

.........................................................................................

.........................................................................................

.........................................................................................

**Reading B**

charge *verb* .......................................................................

flimsy *adjective* ................................................................

billow *verb* ........................................................................

twig *noun* ..........................................................................

hurtle *verb* ........................................................................

wilderness *noun* ...............................................................

solitude *noun* ....................................................................

.........................................................................................

.........................................................................................

.........................................................................................

# Unit 8

**Reading A**

elusive *adjective* ...............................................................

standing *noun* ...................................................................

elude *verb* .........................................................................

offence *noun* .....................................................................

persistent *adjective* ..........................................................

endorse *verb* .....................................................................

obsessive *noun* .................................................................

devote *verb* .......................................................................

portable *adjective* .............................................................

reap rewards *collocation* ...................................................

frame *noun* ........................................................................

manufacturing *noun* ..........................................................

.........................................................................................

.........................................................................................

.........................................................................................

.........................................................................................

**Reading B**

overtake *verb* ....................................................................

psychologist *noun* .............................................................

perception *noun* ................................................................

predictable *adjective* .........................................................

novice *noun* .......................................................................

offender *noun* ...................................................................

wig *noun* ...........................................................................

caution *noun* .....................................................................

fatality *noun* ......................................................................

boom *noun* ........................................................................

hazard *noun* ......................................................................

collision *noun* ...................................................................

outweigh *verb* ...................................................................

.........................................................................................

.........................................................................................

.........................................................................................

# Unit 9

**Reading A**

prevent *verb* ......................................................................

threat *noun* ........................................................................

respect *verb* ......................................................................

lead *noun* ..........................................................................

appliance *noun* ..................................................................

fire exit *noun* .....................................................................

fire door *noun* ...................................................................

fire drill *noun* .....................................................................

fire alarm *noun* ..................................................................

.........................................................................................

.........................................................................................

.........................................................................................

**Reading B**

suspect *verb* ......................................................................

vicinity *noun* ......................................................................

intermittent *adjective* ........................................................

continuous *adjective* .........................................................

vacate *verb* .......................................................................

assembly point *noun* .........................................................

.........................................................................................

.........................................................................................

.........................................................................................

# Unit 10
## Reading A
marketing *noun* _____
folder *noun* _____
ship *verb* _____
cover *verb* _____
canteen *noun* _____
schedule *verb* _____
postpone *verb* _____

## Reading B
emotion *noun* _____
resign *verb* _____
challenge *noun* _____
recruitment *noun* _____
promote *verb* _____
publicity *noun* _____
promotional item *noun* _____
invaluable *adjective* _____
supplier *noun* _____
maternity leave *noun* _____

# Unit 11
## Reading A
post *adjective* _____
vital *adjective* _____
satisfactory *adjective* _____
rate *verb* _____
picnic lunch *noun* _____
criticism *noun* _____
scale *noun* _____
scrutinize *verb* _____
hotelier *noun* _____

## Reading B
feedback *noun* _____
booking *noun* _____
client *noun* _____
food poisoning *noun* _____
aspect *noun* _____
refurbish *verb* _____
remote *adjective* _____

# Unit 12
## Reading A
vacancy *noun* _____
handle *verb* _____
spreadsheet *noun* _____
database *noun* _____
enthusiasm *noun* _____
detail *noun* _____
accuracy *noun* _____
methodical *adjective* _____
initiative *noun* _____
deadline *noun* _____

## Reading B
salary *noun* _____
probationary period *noun* _____
excess *noun* _____
annual leave *noun* _____
entitlement *noun* _____
remuneration *noun* _____
commencement *noun* _____

# Appendix 1 Useful language

## Unit 13

### Reading A

GDP (gross domestic product) *noun* _____

bn (billion) *noun* _____

export *noun* _____

goods *noun* _____

financial services *noun* _____

construction *noun* _____

utilities *noun* _____

machinery *noun* _____

equipment *noun* _____

petroleum products *noun* _____

chemicals *noun* _____

manufactured goods *noun* _____

import *noun* _____

_____

_____

_____

### Reading B

etiquette *noun* _____

bear in mind *expression* _____

status *noun* _____

nickname *noun* _____

handshake *noun* _____

business card *noun* _____

protocol *noun* _____

counterpart *noun* _____

small talk *noun* _____

_____

_____

_____

## Unit 14

### Reading A

thesaurus *noun* _____

encyclopaedia *noun* _____

alphabetical order *noun* _____

idiom *noun* _____

_____

_____

_____

### Reading B

simile *noun* _____

abbreviation *noun* _____

acronym *noun* _____

_____

_____

_____

## Unit 15

### Reading A

catalogue *noun* _____

audio book *noun* _____

search *noun + verb* _____

mouse *noun* _____

return key *noun* _____

keyword *noun* _____

_____

_____

_____

### Reading B

cast *noun* _____

murder *noun* _____

suspect *noun* _____

corpse *noun* _____

strangle *verb* _____

_____

_____

_____

## Unit 16

### Reading A

ability *noun* _____

technique *noun* _____

classify *verb* _____

recreational *adjective* _____

shift *verb* _____

provide *verb* _____

pay (close) attention to *expression* _____

flexibility *noun* _____

pattern *noun* _____

_____

_____

_____

### Reading B

process *noun* _____

memory *noun* _____

unfamiliar *adjective* _____

clue *noun* _____

prefix *noun* _____

suffix *noun* _____

_____

_____

_____

# Appendix 2
# Learning tips

Each unit of this book contains one *Learning tip*. However, this does not mean that this tip is useful in only that particular unit. Most *Learning tips* can be used in several different units. Here are all the *Learning tips* in the book. Each one is under its unit heading and you will also find a list of the types of text you read in that unit.

When you have completed a unit, decide which text you used the *Learning tip* with (this could be more than one text type). In addition, look at the other *Learning tips* and decide if you also used any of those tips in the unit you have just finished. Make a note of the unit name and number and the text type on the empty lines. In this way, you can keep a record of the reading strategies that you are developing.

## Unit1  I'll cook something

### Learning tip

We always read for a purpose. Sometimes this means that we do not need to read everything in front of us in order to find the information we are looking for. We can ignore some of the text.

A  recipes ☐
B  packaging ☐
    till receipt ☐

**Which other units have you used this *Learning tip* in?**

-----------------------------------------------------
-----------------------------------------------------
-----------------------------------------------------

## Unit2  We've hired a car

### Learning tip

We sometimes search a text for a specific piece of information – this could be the answer to a question or simply a particular word or words. This type of reading is called scanning. When we scan, we do not read every word. We look quickly to find what we are looking for.
Scanning may be the first step in our reading of a text. Once we have found something we are looking for, we might go on to read the text around it.

A  car rental voucher ☐
    webpage ☐
B  rental instructions ☐

**Which other units have you used this *Learning tip* in?**

-----------------------------------------------------
-----------------------------------------------------
-----------------------------------------------------

## Unit3  Somewhere to live

### Learning tip

The texts in this book are real texts written for ordinary people. These people read the texts with a purpose in mind – for example, people read accommodation advertisements like those in this unit because they want a place to live.
When you read a text, ask yourself: Who would read this text? Why would they read it? Understanding who would read something, and why, will help you to read the text as if you were reading it in the real world.

A  advertisements ☐
B  tenancy agreement ☐

**Which other units have you used this *Learning tip* in?**

-----------------------------------------------------
-----------------------------------------------------
-----------------------------------------------------

# Appendix 2 Learning tips

## Unit 4 I'll check it in

### Learning tip

We usually look at a text quickly to find out what it is about. This type of reading is called skimming. When we skim, we get the main idea and don't pay attention to the small details. Skimming is very often the first step in reading a text.

A webpage ☐
 webpage ☐
B lost luggage form ☐

**Which other units have you used this *Learning tip* in?**

------------------------------------------------
------------------------------------------------
------------------------------------------------

## Unit 5 I'll be at home

### Learning tip

We often skim a text the first time we read it – we read it quickly to get a general sense. Alternatively, we scan a text – we read it quickly to find a particular piece of information. After a quick read, we sometimes go back and read parts of the text more carefully to find out further, more detailed information. We can use any combination of these different reading skills to find the information we need.

A mail delivery card ☐
 webpage ☐
B leaflet ☐

**Which other units have you used this *Learning tip* in?**

------------------------------------------------
------------------------------------------------
------------------------------------------------

## Unit 6 A weekend in Wales

### Learning tip

Think about what you already know about a topic before you read a text about it. This allows you to relate what you read to what you already know, and it makes the new text easier to understand.

A webpage ☐
B letter ☐

**Which other units have you used this *Learning tip* in?**

------------------------------------------------
------------------------------------------------
------------------------------------------------

## Unit 7 I saw an article about it

### Learning tip

Journalists often begin factual magazine articles with dramatic true stories to catch the reader's attention. They give the factual information later. To tell these true stories, journalists might use direct speech, past tenses and personal pronouns (*I, he, we*, etc.). Look out for these things in an article and then you will be able to recognize which parts of it are the dramatic beginning and which parts give the factual information.

A magazine article ☐
B magazine article ☐

**Which other units have you used this *Learning tip* in?**

------------------------------------------------
------------------------------------------------
------------------------------------------------

## Unit8 **In the newspapers**

### Learning tip

Newspapers contain an enormous number and variety of reading texts, but most people do not read a newspaper from cover to cover. What we read depends on what we are interested in. We look at headlines, which summarize articles, and either read the article – part of it or all of it, again depending on our interest – or move on to another article. We read selectively.

A  beginnings of newspaper articles ☐
B  newspaper article ☐

**Which other units have you used this _Learning tip_ in?**

----------------------------------------------
----------------------------------------------
----------------------------------------------

## Unit9 **Let's go there**

### Learning tip

Dictionaries – both bilingual and monolingual – are very useful when you are learning a language. However, try not to use them too much. When you are reading, try to work out the meaning of an unknown word. Think about the other words around it, the word class it belongs to (e.g. noun, verb), similar words you know in English and similar words in your own language. Then use the dictionary to check that you have worked out the meaning of the word correctly.

A  leaflet ☐
B  notice ☐

**Which other units have you used this _Learning tip_ in?**

----------------------------------------------
----------------------------------------------
----------------------------------------------

## Unit 10 **Lines of communication**

### Learning tip

When you read an email, find out who it is from and who it is for. Sometimes the message is just for you, sometimes it is for you as a member of a group, and sometimes you are copied in (cc = carbon copy, i.e. you are sent a copy of an email which has been sent primarily to someone else). If you know who the email has been sent to, you will know whether you have to reply, or take some kind of action.

A  emails ☐
B  emails ☐
   notices ☐

**Which other units have you used this _Learning tip_ in?**

----------------------------------------------
----------------------------------------------
----------------------------------------------

## Unit 11 **Any comments?**

### Learning tip

Make sure you know the meaning of words and expressions used to link facts and ideas. This will help you to understand the meaning of the text and what the writer is saying. Here are some examples:

| | |
|---|---|
| giving a reason | _because, since, as_ |
| expressing a contrast | _whereas, otherwise, but, while, however, although_ |
| expressing a result | _consequently, therefore, as a result_ |
| rephrasing | _in other words, i.e._ |
| giving an example | _for example, for instance, e.g._ |
| adding something | _furthermore, in addition, also_ |

A  questionnaire ☐
B  report ☐

**Which other units have you used this _Learning tip_ in?**

----------------------------------------------
----------------------------------------------
----------------------------------------------

## Unit 12 I'm going to apply

### Learning tip

Most of our everyday correspondence, such as notes and emails, is in informal language. However, on some occasions we receive formal letters. The language used in these is serious and correct, and less like spoken language. One way of understanding the content of a formal letter is to put it into more neutral everyday language.

A  job advertisement ☐
   part of a CV ☐
B  letter of appointment ☐

**Which other units have you used this *Learning tip* in?**

----

## Unit 13 I'm off on a trip

### Learning tip

We don't only read texts. We also read visuals, such as tables, graphs and diagrams. Often these are a more direct way of presenting information than through text. Visuals sometimes have to be read with text, but at other times they stand alone. As with texts, we always read them with a purpose and that is to extract meaning.

A  webpages ☐
B  webpage ☐

**Which other units have you used this *Learning tip* in?**

----

## Unit 14 Look it up!

### Learning tip

We use reference books for finding specific pieces of information. Each double page of an alphabetically ordered reference book has two words in bold at the top of the pages. These show the first and last entries on those two pages. Our knowledge of the alphabet helps us to scan the reference book to find the words we are looking for.

A  reference book entries ☐
B  introduction to a book of facts ☐
   headings in a book of facts ☐
   entries from a book of facts ☐

**Which other units have you used this *Learning tip* in?**

----

## Unit 15 It's on the shelf

### Learning tip

Reading whole articles, stories and books is a good way to improve your extensive reading skills so that reading for study becomes easier.
When you go to a bookshop or library, choose books that you are interested in. Skim two or three pages and make sure there are not too many new words (a maximum of ten per page). If there are more, you won't be able to work out their meaning from the other words in the text. Direct speech breaks up the text and is generally easier than narrative or descriptive writing.
When you start reading, don't stop in the middle of a sentence or paragraph and go back – continue until the end of a page or chapter.

A  webpages ☐
B  novel extract ☐

**Which other units have you used this *Learning tip* in?**

----

# Unit **16** Read about reading

## Learning tip

When we read a long text for the first time, we usually skim it in order to find out the general meaning and to identify the parts which we want to read in detail. The most important parts of the text are the first paragraph, which introduces the overall topic, and the first sentence of each of the other paragraphs. This sentence usually introduces the topic of the paragraph.

A   encyclopaedia extract   ☐
B   encyclopaedia extract   ☐

**Which other units have you used this _Learning tip_ in?**

---------------------------------------------------------------------
---------------------------------------------------------------------
---------------------------------------------------------------------

# Appendix3
# Using a dictionary

## What kind of dictionary should I use?

If possible, you should use two dictionaries: a good bilingual dictionary (in both your own language and with English translations) and a good monolingual dictionary (English words with English definitions). A monolingual dictionary may give you more information about a word or phrase; in addition, it is a good idea for you to work in English as much as possible. The examples on these pages are from the *Cambridge Learner's Dictionary*.

## What information can I find in a dictionary?

The most common reason for looking a word up in a dictionary is to find out its meaning. However, a dictionary can also give you a lot of other information about a word. The *Cambridge Learner's Dictionary*, for example, can give up to six types of information before the meaning of the word and two further types of information after it. The words in the following examples are all from Unit 1.

1 the base form of the word

> Each entry begins with the base form of the word.

> **yolk** /jəʊk/ *noun* [C] the round, yellow part in the middle of an egg

2 the pronunciation of the word

> These symbols show you how to say the word.

> **sieve** /sɪv/ *noun* [C] a piece of kitchen equipment with a wire or plastic net which separates large pieces of food from liquids or powders *Pass the sauce through a sieve to remove any lumps.* ⟲See colour picture **The Kitchen** on page Centre 2. ● sieve *verb* [T]

3 its part of speech

> This tells you what part of speech – noun, verb, adjective, etc. – a word is.

> **partially** /ˈpɑːʃəli/ *adverb* not completely *partially cooked*

4  any special grammatical features of
   the word

> **[often passive]** shows that the passive
> form (modified) of this verb is often used

> **modify** /'mɒdɪfaɪ/ *verb* [T] **1** to change some-
> thing in order to improve it **[often passive]** *The
> plans will have to be modified to reduce costs.*
> ○ *genetically modified food*

5  irregular past tense forms, plural nouns
   and comparatives/superlatives

> Plurals which are not regular are shown.

> ○━**leaf¹** /liːf/ *noun* [C] *plural* **leaves** /liːvz/ **1** a flat,
> green part of a **plant that grows from a stem
> or branch** *an oak leaf*

6  whether the word is only used in British
   English (UK) or American English (US)

> *UK* means that a word is only used in British English;
> *US* means that a word is used only in American English.

> **aubergine** /'əʊbəʒiːn/ *UK* (*US* **eggplant**) *noun* [C,
> U] an oval, purple vegetable that is white
> inside

7  the meaning of the word

> **packaging** /'pækɪdʒɪŋ/ *noun* [U] the paper, box,
> etc that something is inside so that it can be
> sold or sent somewhere

> The definition tells you
> what the word means.

8  example phrases or sentences

> **roam** /rəʊm/ *verb* [I, T] to move around a place
> without any purpose *gangs of youths roaming
> the street at night*

> Examples (in *italics*) can
> show you how a word is
> used in a phrase/sentence.

9  other words this word goes with (collocations)

> ○━**mix¹** /mɪks/ *verb* **1** COMBINE SUBSTANCES [I, T] If two
> or more substances mix, they combine to
> more substances, you combine them to make
> one substance. *Mix the powder with water to
> form a paste.* ○ *Put the chocolate, butter, and
> egg in a bowl and mix them all together.*

> Words in **bold** in an example show you
> which words are often used together.

## How should I use my dictionary?

1   At the top of each page in the *Cambridge Learner's Dictionary*, there is a word in **bold** black type. The word in the top left corner of the left page is the first word on this page; the word in the top right corner of the right page is the last word on this page. If you are looking for the word **sponge**, it will be between the two words **split** (top left corner of the left page) and **spread** (top right corner of the right page).

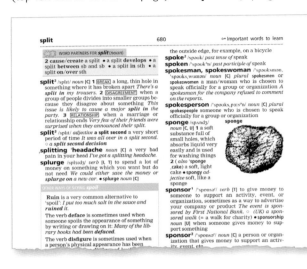

split    680    ◦▪ Important words to learn

◦▪ Important words to learn    681    spread

2   Each time you look up a word, you could use a highlighter pen to mark the word in your dictionary. When you return to a page with a highlighter mark, look at the word quickly and check that you remember its meaning.

**savour** UK (US **savor**) /'seɪvəʳ/ *verb* [T] to enjoy food or a pleasant experience as much and as slowly as possible *to savour a meal* ◦ *I ate slowly, savouring every mouthful.* ◦ *We savoured our moment of victory.*

**savoury** UK (US **savory**) /'seɪvʳri/ *adjective* Savoury food is not sweet. *savoury biscuits* ◦ *Generally, I prefer savoury to sweet food.*

**savvy** /'sævi/ *noun* [U] *informal* practical knowledge and ability *business/political savvy* • **savvy** *adjective informal* having knowledge and ability *a savvy consumer*

3   A word in your dictionary may not be exactly the same as its form in the text you are reading. This is because the word in the text may be: a plural form of a noun; a comparative or superlative form of an adjective; a verb ending in *-s*, *-ed*, *-ing*; or an irregular form of a verb, e.g. *minced*.

**mince**[1] /mɪns/ UK (US **ground beef**) *noun* [U] meat, usually from a cow, which has been cut into very small pieces by a machine

**mince**[2] /mɪns/ *verb* [T] to cut food into small pieces in a machine *minced beef/onions*

**mincemeat** /'mɪnsmiːt/ *noun* [U] **1** a spicy, sweet mixture of apples, dried fruit, and nuts, which have been cut into small pieces **2 make mincemeat of sb** *informal* to defeat someone very easily

**mince 'pie** *noun* [C] UK a small pastry filled with mincemeat that is eaten mainly at Christmas

4 The words that are defined in the dictionary are called headwords. Sometimes a headword can have more than one meaning. The first meaning in the dictionary is not always the one you want. Read through the different meanings and decide which one is correct in this context.

A headword is the word whose meaning is explained.

**clove** /kləʊv/ *noun* [C] **1** a small, dark-brown, dried flower that is used as a spice **2** one separate part in a root of garlic (= plant with a strong taste used in cooking)

A guideword helps you find the meaning you want.

**grain** /greɪn/ *noun* **1** SEED [C, U] a seed or seeds from types of grass which are eaten as food *grains of wheat/rice* **2** PIECE [C] a very small piece of something *a grain of sand/sugar* **3** QUALITY [no plural] a very small amount of a quality *There isn't a grain of truth in her story.* **4 the grain** the natural direction and pattern of lines which you can see in wood or material *to cut something along/against the grain* **5 go against the grain** If something goes against the grain, you would not normally do it because it would be unusual or morally wrong. ⊃See also: take sth with a pinch of **salt¹**.

5 Words which have several meanings sometimes have guidewords to help you find the meaning you are looking for. Usually the most common meaning appears first. The first meaning in the dictionary is not always the one you want. Read through the different meanings and decide which one is correct in this context.

6 Some words in your dictionary may have more than one headword. (Small numbers after the headword will indicate this.) This is because the word can be used as different parts of speech – for example, an adjective and a noun. The part of speech of the unknown word should be clear from the context (the words around it).

○–**medium¹** /ˈmiːdiəm/ *adjective* in the middle of a group of different amounts or sizes *people of medium weight* ○ *She bought a medium-sized car.* ○ *The shirt comes in small, medium, and large.*
**medium²** /ˈmiːdiəm/ *noun* [C] *plural* **media** or **mediums** a way of communicating or expressing something *the medium of television/radio* ○ *The Internet has become yet another medium for marketing.*

7 Dictionaries are particularly helpful with the meaning of phrasal verbs and idioms since their meaning is different from the meaning of the separate parts. You will find phrasal verbs, idioms and other expressions after all the other definitions of the word.

## When should I use my dictionary?

A dictionary is very useful when you are learning a foreign language. However, when you are reading, do not use your dictionary too much. Using your dictionary will interrupt your reading and slow you down. In your own language, you don't always understand the meaning of every word; it is not necessary to understand everything in English either.

1 When you see an English word that you don't know, first try to guess the meaning of the word from its context (the words around it). You may find another word with a similar meaning, a word which means the opposite, or some words which actually explain the unknown word. Only use your dictionary to check your guess.

2 The only other time you should look a word up in your dictionary is if there are no clues in the text and you are sure the unknown word is important.